D0504329

# BORIS CHRISTOFF

# BORIS CHRISTOFF

## An Authorized Biography

by Atanas Bozhkoff
Translated by John Woodward

Foreword by LORD HAREWOOD

Edited with a critical discography by
Alan Blyth

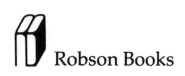 Robson Books

First published in Great Britain in 1991 by
Robson Books Ltd, Bolsover House,
5–6 Clipstone Street, London W1P 7EB

Text copyright © 1991 Atanas Bozhkoff
Critical discography copyright © 1991 Alan Blyth

**British Library Cataloguing in Publication Data**

Bozhkoff, Atanas
 Boris Christoff.
 1. Opera. Singing. Christoff, Boris, 1914–
 I. Title    II. Boris Khristov. *English*
 782.1092

 ISBN 0 86051 731 4

All rights reserved. No part of this
publication may be reproduced, stored in a
retrieval system, or transmitted in any form
or by any means, electronic, mechanical,
photocopying, recording or otherwise,
without the prior permission in writing of
the publishers.

Photoset in North Wales by
Derek Doyle & Associates, Mold, Clwyd.
Printed and bound in Great Britain by
WBC Print Ltd and WBC Bookbinders Ltd,
Bridgend, Glamorgan.

# Contents

# Editor's Note

The main section of this book derives from a biography by a friend of the subject, originally written in Bulgarian for a Bulgarian audience. It has been shortened and somewhat adapted for a more cosmopolitan readership, but inevitably there remain references and details that are slanted towards a more local public. It is not intended as a definitive biography but as a subjective portrait of a much-loved singer. Lord Harewood and I, who both attended a great number of performances given by the singer, have attempted to assess Christoff's career from a more central viewpoint in our respective Foreword and Critical Discography. More than anything the many portraits will remind Christoff's admirers of his greatness as an artist and, with the help of the bass's many discs, perhaps inform younger opera enthusiasts why Christoff is so revered. I would like to acknowledge the invaluable help of John T. Hughes in the editing of the text, of John Woodward of the BBC Bulgarian Service for his translation, and of Cecilia Gobbi for her encouragement.

A.B.

# Foreword by Lord Harewood

I first heard Boris Christoff early in 1949 at La Scala in, of all operas, *Fidelio*, when I had no impression of a heavy Germanic bass (the opera was sung in Italian, with singers like Delia Rigal, Mirto Picchi and Giuseppe Taddei in the cast), but rather of an artist of peculiar intensity and interest. Another hearing only a matter of months later at Covent Garden as *Boris Godunov* confirmed, or rather transformed, that first impression. This was obviously a great operatic performer – the singing on a generous scale, incisive and always expressive, the whole characterization carefully shaped, from the remarkably controlled *mezza voce* of the Coronation scene to the equally well-controlled yet grandiose climax of the Death: an artist of the highest quality.

Some 40 years later, I have heard nothing from Christoff to change my mind. Year after year came new roles, new recordings, the occasional recital. I knew from an *Ernani* in Rome, a Procida in Florence, that his singing of Verdi was supremely good because of virtues that had been apparent from the start: the clean attack, the insistence on a strong singing line, the lean beauty of the voice itself, the conviction he brought to every element of performance. But even to those of us who were already convinced that this was an artist of rare calibre, his Philip II in *Don Carlos* at Covent Garden in 1958, with Giulini conducting and in Visconti's production, came as a revelation. The cast was magnificent, honed by a great conductor and producer, about as close to perfection as most of us are likely to see and hear, and each member seemed to be demonstrating the quintessence of his or her operatic possibilities. Quite apart from attributes of majesty and command which the role of Philip postulates, Christoff in the first scene of Act IV showed a sense of isolation, of being at the eye of the storm, a stillness, which became in some ways the climax of the opera; a stillness of singing, of course, but also of movement, so that when just before the end of the monologue he rose from his chair for the ·first time, it was as if decisions had been taken which would shake empires and human lives to the end of the earth. If I remember just as vividly the rolling bass line beneath the quartet later in the same scene, that is because this artist was a great Verdian singer as well as a great solo performer.

Christoff is often too narrowly categorized as an operatic tragedian; there was more to him than that, more versatility, more musical ground carefully and rewardingly tilled. I caught his Prince Galitsky and Khan Konchak in *Prince Igor* in Rome quite early in his career, and knew from the former why he had wanted to sing Varlaam in *Boris Godunov* as well as Boris in his recordings; from the latter how crucial to Russian operas is that sardonic strain which seems to come more naturally to Slav singers than to any others. I marvelled at his singing of Gurnemanz in *Parsifal*, again at La Scala, when his gestures of penitence as he knelt late in the first act made others seem perfunctory in their prayer. I revelled in the economy of his Don Basilio in Edinburgh in 1961, which I remember Benjamin Britten pin-pointing as the essence of comedy timing in music – because he did so little. I admired (and, on his marvellous recording, continue to enjoy) the wide range of his characterization in Mussorgsky songs. I doubt whether I have ever heard a bass in the Verdi Requiem create such a sense of awe and expectation as when he sang it in Salzburg with Herbert von Karajan over 40 years ago.

Now he has retired, and this chronicle of his achievement, written by a fellow Bulgarian, is appearing in English. It seems like the end of an era, but I remind myself that Christoff, like Callas, in those two decades from 1950 redefined and illuminated certain areas of the repertory, so that later singers approach them in a way he has opened up, and audiences listen with ears sharpened by his very particular, very powerful perceptions.

# 1

## *Secrets of the Family Tree*

Those who heard Christo Psalta – the grandfather of the world-famous bass – said that when he sang 'even the nightingales fell silent in order to listen to him'. A charming conceit, but there is no doubting the depth of admiration of those who heard the singing of the 'first cantor' of the independent Bulgarian church in Vitolya, Christoff's home town in Macedonia.

Boris Christoff's father, Kiril, was one of the exemplars of the church. He had studied literature in France and became a teacher in a gymnasium, but later the family's musical traditions deeply influenced the whole of his life. As well as all his other religious duties, he sang as a soloist at church and at civil ceremonies, and he collected Bulgarian folk songs from Macedonia. Later, members of the Institute of Musicology at the Bulgarian Academy of Sciences recorded his performances of more than 300 ancient folk songs.

Christoff's mother, Raina Todorova Popivanova, had the

strong will, quick mind and sense of order so necessary for the development of her son's talent. Her ability to manage the family budget and her sense of responsibility – she carried the keys of the house upon her breast 'like a monastery housekeeper' – were the normal qualities and habits of a Bulgarian woman of that time. Friends recall that she attended a business school. They remember also that her father – Grandfather Todor – had been a pilgrim, that he loved singing, and that Boris received from him a piece of the 'holy cross' he had brought back from the holy places.

The house on Tsar Samuil Street in Sofia in which Raina Todorova and Kiril Christoff first lived was a tumbledown single-storey building, hidden modestly inside a courtyard. Later the young family built a new house on the street itself. Although a master-builder and workmen were engaged for the task, the house was built on Raina's initiative and to her design. Perhaps she was influenced by the Bulgarian's traditionally powerful attachment to a house which he has built and which he will rarely willingly leave or replace. Or perhaps it was a presentiment that she was to be responsible for everything which took place in this house.

Boris was born in Plovdiv, some 90 miles south-east of Sofia, where his father was briefly a teacher at a school. Some kind of military celebration was being marked on 18 May 1914, and when Boris was born at eight o'clock that morning the boom of guns echoed over Plovdiv. Kiril Christoff recalled telling his wife, 'Raina, you have given birth to an important son. He has arrived to a gun salute.' Boris's later development had few connections with the city – though music lovers may recall that somewhere here, on the banks of the ancient Khebra, Orpheus lamented his Eurydice.

Boris considered No. 43 Tsar Samuil Street in Sofia to be

not only his maternal home but also his birthplace. It played a particularly important role in his spiritual and creative development, and all his happiest childhood experiences were associated with it. The house was his first school, at least so far as ethics, courage and even theatre are concerned, and it was the first place in which he encountered people he could trust. It was visited by Sofronniy, the Metropolitan of Tŭrnovo, who was a magnificent singer and a friend of Kiril's. It was visited by people who were involved in the revolutionary struggle in Macedonia.

Kiril Christoff had studied at Dedéagach (the modern Greek port of Alexandroúpolis) from 1896 to 1900 and had become imbued with the ideals of the Bulgaria of the Treaty of San Stefano. Later he was chairman of the Ilinden organization, a political and cultural association, for 15 years. It is easy to understand what this meant to him, particularly in view of the coups and internal conflicts among the various factions. Making use of the knowledge he had gained during his student days in France, and by now a teacher and civil servant in Sofia, he played an important part in setting up the trade school on Slivnitsa Boulevard, and it was on his initiative that evening classes to fight illiteracy were set up in the capital. These initiatives and contacts naturally expanded his circle of acquaintances, and he was close to many people who contributed to the cultural life and choral art of the country, and this enriched the home life of the family.

One day during Lent at the beginning of the 1920s an unusual trio performed at the house in Tsar Samuil Street. It consisted of Kiril Christoff, a civil servant friend, Lazar, and Metropolitan Sofronniy. The informal concert of songs lasted the whole day. The child Boris listened outside the door and at one point, when he peeped through the keyhole, it seemed to him that his father was weeping with joy.

Boris was not yet 10 years old when, in neighbouring Bystritsa Street, a choir and balalaika orchestra were formed, and enthusiasts from the whole district joined. The initiator was a Russian émigré officer, Konstantin Chernov, a wonderful singer and balalaika player who inspired many young people with a love for Russian music. At this stage the young Boris only listened and absorbed, but his interest in the musical heritage he was later to interpret with such brilliant insight had already been born, and grew apace when the group began to play and sing at parties at the Christoffs' house.

Boris's elder brother Nikolai was also a singer who played in the orchestra and composed some pieces for it. The brothers were very close, sharing many friends and exploring the world of music together.

When, as an internationally famous singer, he reflected on his boyhood, Christoff saw his family home as an academy of his development and a treasure-house of his feelings. Everything in his adult life was connected with it. His greatest love, despite his studies in law and history, has always been the arts. That love was nurtured and developed in his childhood home, for which he retained a great affection. Here, alongside the splinter of the 'holy cross' from Grandfather Todor, are the pictures which first attracted him to art: a wonderful sketch in oils of horses by Pencho Georgiev and a small watercolour depicting a medieval warrior, which later served as a model for his Attila. Here, too, his brother taught him how to sing those heartfelt Russian songs that later so moved those who flocked to his concerts and collected his recordings.

Many years later, he proposed the construction of new buildings in the yard of this house with rooms for storing pictures, theatrical costumes, records and television films;

with classrooms seating 15–20 people; with a small experimental theatre and a huge library. The proposal, addressed to the leaders of education and art in Sofia, explained that he would freely donate his entire property and would contribute both morally and materially to the creation of a new school for singers. The government has recently taken action and the house shall be a municipal music school.

In 1967, a few days after his mother's death, he talked to a lawyer friend in Sofia about the complications of inheritance, complications not so much financial and legal as moral. His mother had dreamed about opening the doors of the house to the education of new talents, and had deposited her will with the court. On 8 February 1971, Christoff wrote a new and more detailed letter, this time to the mayor of Sofia: 'Inspired by the desire to serve as an example of a dignified Bulgarian and to be remembered by future Bulgarian generations, by the Slavs, and by mankind in general for my deeds, and following the examples set by my parents and my brother, who were the best breeding-ground on which I developed my qualities as a person, artist and patriot, I have decided, as the last living representative of my family, to donate with immediate effect the property I have inherited in Sofia to the Sofia city council for the creation of an institute for the most talented young Bulgarians in the field of singing and operatic art ....'

Boris Christoff started singing late. At home he studied the violin and the guitar, but for a long time he made no attempt at singing, at least in front of the others. His father even seemed to be a bit concerned: would he forsake the family tradition? In fact, Boris had already taken his first steps in singing as a member of the children's choir, the Sofia Nightingales. But these first steps seem to have gone largely unnoticed, and later his high-school teachers did not discover his exceptional talent at once. His contemporaries at the Second Male Gymnasium recall that he did well. They remember his curiosity, his clear memory and his burgeoning musical gifts; and much later, when preparations to celebrate the centenary of the school were under way, they did not forget to invite him. Even as late as the beginning of the 1930s, however, Boris was still getting indifferent marks from his singing teacher.

And then the sudden transformation occurred. One evening, approaching their home along the quiet Tsar Samuil Street, his parents heard through the open windows of the house a voice singing with a magnificent timbre. The singer was their son Boris. His friends were also able to appreciate the startling voice and they were soon listening to him with admiration as he sang Russian songs and romances. As for the singing teacher, from that moment on he made Boris the soloist in the school choir.

Other factors, too, brought about changes in the boy. He matured under influences which his teachers condescendingly described as youthful fancies. On one occasion the geography teacher took his class to Yumrukchal, the mountain zone in Bulgarian Macedonia. In a voice trembling with excitement he talked about Macedonia and the desperate struggle fought for its liberation. Boris's eyes filled with tears as he associated what he heard with what he had been told about his homeland by his father. His carefree wanderings around the quarters of Sofia and his days spent camping in the valley of the Vladaya river brought him experiences and relationships that would help to develop his national awareness and sympathy for the ordinary people. In this environment the songs became more and more serious, as his attitude towards singing became more personal, wiser and more active.

This was based on a quickly developing sense of reality and truth, helped by an increasing concern with theatrical interpretation. Not surprisingly, even at this early stage, he became associated with the Staro Bulgarski Tserkovni Peyaniya (Ancient Bulgarian Church Singing) circle. He has since recalled the informal recital given at home by his father, Metropolitan Sofronniy and their friend Lazar. He was attracted to them not only because of their heartfelt songs but also because of their laughter and recollections of their youth in the Macedonian-Odrin resistance. Other important factors in the awakening of Boris's vocal talents were his first visits to the opera and his meetings with singers such as the then well-known baritone Tsetan Korolev (1890–1960). The impact of these contacts, which took place when he was a student in the fifth and sixth classes, was, he said, tremendous. The first Sunday matinée which he attended – of Weber's *Der Freischütz* – was decisive: his romantic imagination was captured for ever by the riveting world of opera. That was followed by visits to *Boris Godunov* and the excitement at the art of Evgeny Zhdanovski; then to *Madama Butterfly*, in which he heard the voice of Vanya Levento; and then to *Carmen*, in which Ilka Popova bewitched him with her deep mezzo-soprano.

This favourable course of events was due to the tact and the personal example of his father – a fact warmly acknow-ledged by Boris then and later. His father, who was also his friend and adviser, died on 25 September 1961. Because of visa problems, Boris was unable to attend the funeral, the service for which was held at the Sveta Nedelya cathedral. So many people had gathered that the church was packed. After the absolution, the floor was taken by the Bulgarian Patriarch Kyril, who praised the exemplary life of the deceased, his modesty and his virtues as a husband, father and public figure.

On learning of his father's death, Christoff had sent a telegram to his mother from Rome:

Mother mine,
A dreadful mourning grips my heart for my dear, sweet, lamented father, and I am so sad that I am unable to come because of lack of the appropriate documents, so sad that I cannot embrace and kiss him in a last farewell. I beg you on my knees, my dear only mother, do not despair; I shall come soon. As a last farewell to my dear father I beseech you to embrace him for me and kiss his holy forehead.
    Your loving son Boris.

Another telegram, sent a little later, included the words he would have pronounced at his father's death-bed. A close friend from his youth, Lyubin Zhivkov, read them out and then placed the telegram, together with a rose, in the hands of the deceased.

When he left the Gymnasium in 1932, Boris faced a choice. His mother, apprehensive about the difficulties of an artistic career, advised him to go to the Faculty of Law at the university, as his brother Nikolai had done, rather than to the music academy. And that is what he did, but as he was completing his higher education as a lawyer he did not believe he had found his place in life and felt no desire to make use of his diploma. Having completed his university course, he continued to acquire for himself musical scores, rather than legal books. He had already sung in the Gusla Choir and in the Academic Choir, and afterwards joined the Alexander Nevsky Cathedral choir in Sofia. For him this was a new school and one of far greater importance than his university education. In the 1930s the choral movement in Bulgaria encompassed hundreds of enthusiastic singers and had a fruitful influence on the musical culture of the nation. The preferred style of *a capella* singing provided a great opportunity for the development of brilliant soloists, and Boris Christoff, with his pronounced taste for church singing, was also influenced by it. In the choir of the Alexander Nevsky he met people who were wholeheartedly devoted to the cause, notably Dobri Christoff, the conductor of the choir, and Angel Popkonstantinov, his assistant.

He became increasingly involved in the concert activity of the choirs, and the extraordinary capacity of his voice was making an increasingly greater impression. Many of his friends encouraged him to continue his studies, perhaps with a teacher in Italy, although he himself was still wavering, and reacted to all this advice with painful uncertainty.

In 1933 Boris Christoff joined the noted Gusla Choir. He had to pass a competitive entrance examination which at that time was as difficult as entering the opera. The conductor of the choir was Professor Assen Dimitrov (1894–1960), who was greatly impressed by Christoff's performance at the examination and later told him: 'You have to thank heaven. You must dedicate yourself to singing. You have to learn. You have a talent which will take you to the heights, to be the pride of Bulgaria. Otherwise – on your own head be it!' Founded in 1929, with Christo Manolov as its first conductor, the Gusla was one of the best amateur choirs in the country during the 1930s and early 1940s. It received no support from the state, but maintained a high artistic level which won it a rare reputation. An ambition to reach a thoroughly professional standard was shared by all the singers, and was in fact a condition of membership. In consequence the Gusla had a rich and full artistic life despite its amateur status. Its 90-strong membership altered a great deal through the years but its prestige remained unchanged.

It began to achieve success abroad in the 1930s: Italy 1932, Hungary 1933, Austria 1936, Poland 1937 and Germany 1940. In 1932 the Italian newspaper *Il Popolo* wrote, 'Gusla's concerts are an impressive manifestation of a great choral art,' adding that the choir 'contains beautiful, clear, powerful and flexible voices.' When the choir met Christoff years later, after he had achieved world fame, its members did not feel like poor relations in his presence. Nor did he allow himself to look down on them, and every time he returned to Bulgaria he sang with them. Indeed, the choir would meet him on his arrival at Sofia airport and later would see him off on his departure abroad, invariably with the words 'Rodna pesen nas navek ni cversva' ('A common song unites us forever'). The people of Sofia became accustomed to that airport ritual – a symbol of what Gusla contributed to the creation of Christoff, something which he cherishes and never forgets.

In January 1933 the Modern Music Society was founded, with the declared aim of creating a Bulgarian national style, and of defending the same principles on which, 14 years earlier, the artists' society National Culture had been founded. The people who headed this new professional organization and set out its guidelines had sufficient experience of the broad European musical traditions to be able to offer new and wide views on the ways in which Bulgarian music might develop.

One of the leading members of the Modern Music Society, Lyubomir Pipkov, who had become something of a cult figure for the young talent in the capital after his return from Paris, wrote that 'The national musical style strikes a blow against the idea of a common European culture, because it is a bridge between the primitive and the contemporary.' According to him a broader view had to be adopted because 'striving towards a national musical culture can be justified only if we have the right appreciation of the international language and meaning of music'. A battle had to be waged 'against the danger of producing a local and too inflexible criterion for art'.

These ideas had a particular significance for Christoff's cultural and artistic flowering and also for his entire development later on. He sang in the Gusla Choir during the period when music of all periods was being attempted within a distinct national style. Composers such as Petko Stainov, Dimiter Nenov and Marin Goleminov were specially commissioned to write songs for the Gusla. Dobri Christoff composed his outstanding songs 'Ergen Dyado' (Old Man Bachelor) and 'Tenka Dafino' (Slim Girl) specially for the choir. Absorbed in the atmosphere of these songs, Christoff, as the Gusla's soloist, was becoming immersed in creative truths that would never fade. For him the Bulgarian national style could not be formed in response to one period alone. It had to be illumined by rays reflecting significant facets of the life of the nation through the centuries and back to the mysteries of ancient times. Those who agreed with him were not surprised when later he continued to support those composers whose songs he sang in the Gusla.

In 1975 Christoff suggested that *Nestinarka* by Marin Goleminov should be produced on the stage of Covent Garden and other major opera houses throughout the world. Some time in 1976, when a plan for a tour by the Sofia National Opera to Bari, Bologna and Florence was being discussed, he spoke persuasively in favour of the company arriving in Italy with only a few works, of which *Nestinarka* would be the chief. His approach to the recording of ancient church chants shows similar understanding. In the preparations for his recording of 'Domestic Liturgy' by Grechaninov (see Discography), he made it clear that he discovered in it traces of the mysteries of pre-Christian culture. At the same time he addressed the problem of modernizing the heritage of past centuries, including religious motifs, with a remarkable understanding and consistency.

When he left for the West, his friends told him he 'was going to learn'. In fact, he was leaving behind in Sofia one of the soundest schools. In the final analysis, the brilliance of a talent is to be found not only in technique but in the depth of its artistic understanding. In the Gusla Choir Christoff had penetrated the depths of his country's musical tradition.

University was followed by military service. Time spent with the military seldom provides anything new in the life of an artist, but in the case of Christoff this was not so. He served in the reserve officers' squadron of the First Cavalry regiment in Sofia and has vivid recollections of the comradeship and shared military discomforts. He remembers an incident in a Sofia café one Sunday while he was on leave when he drew his sword and attacked a policeman who was mistreating a pauper. Christoff and several others were arrested. But army life had its compensations. At his initiative a choir was formed in the regiment; he became its soloist, and the group enjoyed considerable local popularity.

After military service, he graduated as a lawyer and began practical work. He was sent to the town of Pazardjik, and soon he had to plead for the passing of a death sentence on a prisoner – something that gave rise to a great conflict within him. The case was one of premeditated murder with a stolen gun; a young man of seventeen had been killed. When his broken-hearted mother spoke, Christoff felt faint. To whom should one listen in such a situation? Cicero reasoned that 'the law is our judge'; Victor Hugo asserted that 'a law that kills is not a law but a crime'.

Afterwards Christoff managed to get a transfer back to Sofia. But here, too, he was a junior in the prosecutor's department and continued to be faced with painful moral dilemmas. In the capital, however, he was at least in familiar surroundings; and there was the comradeship of his friends and their shared love of music.

In these years when he was reconsidering his values, his intimates (lawyers, painters, intellectuals, civil servants), all of whom loved singing, turned the Kazaka, a tavern on Vitoshka Street, into a centre for their freedom-loving feelings. How better to escape their cares? It was in the Kazaka that they spent a memorable evening of song with the famous Italian soprano Toti Dal Monte after her concert in the Bulgaria Hall in 1938 with the baritone Luigi Montesanto. She had been particularly impressed with Christoff's rich voice, had declared 'he has a soul and imagination' and advised him 'to take the correct path'. Montesanto said he was happy to have discovered 'a remarkable talent! A young man by the name of Christoff, who has a naturally trained voice. How many of the tortures of the black art will he be spared? He only has to grow and mature as an artist.' In such a milieu, it was easier to face his personal problems and to confront his doubts about the future – in particular whether he could dare think of Italy and a career in opera.

Christoff's solo performances at concerts given by the Gusla choir were evidence of his popularity among the serious-minded people and active singers of Sofia, but older members of the Gusla choir were disconcerted by his reserve and shyness. For a long time the choir's director, Assen Dimitrov, was unable to persuade him to sing solos. It was

one of the few occasions when the members of the choir
practically had to use force to bring forward one of their
colleagues. None of them accepts that there was anything
premeditated in this or that his outlook was fatalistic.
Christoff himself has no explanation for his own reserve and
modesty, but he does not conceal the fact that he was afraid.
In 1940 he appeared at a concert in the Bulgaria Hall as a
soloist, singing the song 'Oh, wide steppe'. The audience
showed every sign of boundless enjoyment and gave him a
rapturous reception, calling for three encores and wanting
still more. He, however, was unable to decide whether this
applause was a reward for his talent or for overcoming his
fear! At the start of the 1960s, when he once again appeared
in the Bulgaria Hall, at the entrance he reminded his friend
Lyuben Zhivkov: 'Do you remember how much fear there
was?' Clearly what he had most surely in mind was the fear
of failure. Moreover, in 1940 there were people who
asserted that to perform the song 'Oh, wide steppe'
amounted to promoting Soviet propaganda.

  These waverings were finally, almost suddenly overcome.
At the beginning of the 1940s the chamber choir of the
Royal Chapel, which had been set up as an elite group by the
talented musician Nikolai Nikolayev, consisted of the
sweet-voiced priest, Rafail Alekseyevich, his son, Georgi,
who also had a fine voice, and Angel Popkonstantinov. They
insisted that Boris Christoff should become a member of the
choir. He appeared very rarely in the chapel, but on 19
January 1942, at the traditional service in the square in front
of the Royal Palace and in the presence of the Tsar Boris, the
Tsarina Giovanna, the diplomatic corps and the military
high command, something occurred that everyone noted. It
was terribly cold (18 degrees below zero), and after the
service in the open air everyone was invited into the palace

for a snack and to recover. However, those present had been enchanted with the choir's skill and would not let them stop singing. It was suggested that the choir sing some secular songs. Popkonstantinov had expected some such development and had warned Boris Christoff that he must finish with 'The Song of Nikifor'. Of course, this warning did not have a calming effect and the agitated soloist 'hid' himself somewhere in the back row. The accompanist struck up the tune, his colleagues pushed him forward and formed a semi-circle around him and he began to sing.

Christoff knew this traditional song from the evening gatherings at the Kazaka tavern. It had been performed there first by Georgi, the son of Father Rafail, and Assen Dimitrov, and had been arranged for a mixed choir. Now in the palace it seemed even more moving than in the bohemian club, and after his performance the applause was tempestuous. Christoff remembers that moment: everyone congratulated him. The Tsar and Tsarina were enthusiastic about his singing and asked what new roles he was studying for and were most surprised to hear that he was a lawyer and that he did not have the opportunity to complete his education as a singer.

The admiration of the Tsar and the generous scholarship to study in Italy that he granted to Christoff thoroughly changed the course of his life. After this events moved quickly. His friends saw this official recognition as inevitable, the reward for his talent, his perseverance and the reputation of the Gusla Choir. With the help of his brother Nikolai, he persuaded his father to give his blessing to his Italian adventure; but his mother was devastated: 'Is this how it is? Was not Nikolai the singer?' she exclaimed. 'Goodness, how things have turned out. The lawyer is going away to sing and the singer remains behind.' Everyone knew that these were words of maternal concern and love; and behind the concern were unshakeable hopes for the well-being of her son. Many years later, when friends talked with her, she would say: 'From him I want only one thing, now and in the future: that he should sing and record the most beautiful Bulgarian church music.' Before Christoff's departure the secretary of the Gusla Choir, the lawyer Lyuben Zhivkov, one of Boris's closest friends, wrote a letter to Beniamino Gigli, asking him to listen to their friend and if possible to help him. So that the letter should be more persuasive, the members of the choir ordered a *gusla* (the Bulgarian name for the rebeck, an ancient stringed instrument), which they sent with other presents along with the letter. Finally, by tradition, the members of the choir set up a long table in the Bulgaria restaurant in Sofia for Boris's celebratory send-off – an unforgettably youthful party that went on for two days and two nights.

Christoff decided to leave on 18 May 1942. Early that morning he went to the railway station and bought a ticket for the sleeping-car. The moment of departure was painful for every member of his family, but most especially for his mother. 'Borko,' she said, 'you were born on this day. May God protect you, I have done everything for you. I gave birth to you and I have looked after you. And now you are leaving. Take care and think about yourself. Do not forget us. There is a war on; everything is ablaze.'

That evening, when he saw Boris off at the station, his brother Nikolai was in lieutenant's uniform. The uncertainty, the presentiment of a long parting and the feeling that something valuable had gone from their circle for ever, made their words ponderous and uneven. Just before the train left, Nikolai took out a clover-leaf-shaped pendant which bore the image of Raphael's Sistine Madonna, and hung it around his brother's neck. Christoff has carried the Madonna to this day.

# 2

## The Time Before Dawn

When Boris Christoff set off for Italy the whole of Europe had been turned into a military front and the roads to the future seemed blocked at every turn. For him, however, the course was set.

He arrived in Rome without knowing what sort of reception he could expect, but his first meetings with two legendary artists were encouraging. He sang before Gigli and Pertile, the two great tenors, who found that his voice was 'unusually rich' but needed help through study. Gigli recommended Christoff to a friend of his in Milan who was a teacher. Unfortunately Christoff and this teacher did not get on, and he soon returned to Rome. Shortly afterwards, with the help of an acquaintance at the Bulgarian embassy, he was able to appear before the great baritone Giuseppe De Luca. He sang Boris Godunov's great monologue, and from that moment things changed for the better. De Luca thought highly of his voice and musicality and sent him to study with yet another noted singer, the baritone Riccardo Stracciari, promising to check on his progress from time to time. A period of intense work and of happy collaboration now began, for Stracciari quickly took to his pupil. Stracciari had an only son who had been a good painter but who had died. His sense of loss was eased by this new contact. Christoff sang for him at his home at 25 Corso Trieste every day except Thursday and Sunday, the lessons lasting for about half an hour. The first classes were devoted to familiar musical phrases, suitable for the development of the voice, and were always accompanied by the admonition 'do not sing too loudly'.

Stracciari was well known in Italian musical circles. Born in Bologna in 1875, he had been one of the world's foremost baritones, noted particularly for his portrayal of Figaro (in *The Barber of Seville*) and Rigoletto. The colour, range and power of his voice were legendary (they can still be heard on record) and Christoff drew both inspiration and instruction from these qualities. Stracciari also had the ability to outline a clear plan of systematic study, to inspire respect for work, and to augment a natural enthusiasm for art with the experience he had accumulated since he had begun to teach in 1937. No doubt it was under his influence that Christoff recognized that the classics must not only be loved but also must be vigorously defended against poor taste, financial calculation or misguided innovation on the part of their interpreters. His career bears testimony to the depth of his conviction.

Unfortunately, just as this association was developing, it was violently cut short. Rome had been declared an Open City, but the Allies were already breaking through its defences. There was fighting in the streets and bombs were falling. Christoff held out for a time, but soon the necessary funds for his flat, Italian lessons and daily needs no longer arrived. In September 1943 he felt obliged to return to Bulgaria. Stracciari learnt of his decision too late to be able to help. He got in touch with a member of the Bulgarian embassy in Rome and poured out his distress: 'Where is that young man? Find him, and use the police to bring him back! Do you know what you are losing? He is exceptional. His talents must not be lost: he belongs to the world....'

Meanwhile, Christoff had managed to get back to Sofia after overcoming amazing obstacles in the war-torn Balkans. There, things seemed to have calmed down and he was soon invited to take part in a concert on Radio Sofia, accompanied by Assen Dimitrov. Fortunately, one recording of this concert survived, and more than 30 years later Christoff managed to add it to his collection.

On 13 November 1943, Christoff once again set off for the West, this time to Salzburg. His immersion in the classics of German music had begun. It was at this time that he was drawn towards German song, which he would later perform with such skill in dozens of concerts devoted to the works of Brahms, Schubert and Schumann. But the Axis powers had no need of chamber concerts at this time. What they needed were people who could shoot, and so the authorities tried to make a soldier out of Christoff. He did not become one because his conscience rebelled so strongly against violence and cruelty that he refused to join the corps of Bulgarians fighting on behalf of Germany. As a result he found himself in the Brederis labour camp near Feldkirch.

Christoff bravely endured his heavy lot and waited stoically for the arrival of the Allied forces. He worked alongside young people and children, brought for the most part from the Ukraine. One day the camp greeted the dawn with a host of hammer-and-sickle flags. Several of the children were severely beaten, and it is said that one of them nearly died. A Bulgarian prisoner collected him and began to take care of him, but this aroused suspicion. Moreover, after some of the children managed to escape across the nearby Swiss border he was threatened with death.

On excursions to the village Christoff chanced to meet a girl, an acquaintance of his from Vienna, who was an unsuccessful singer. It happened that her brother was commandant of the camp. She was, however, too frightened to do anything to ease his lot, and her brother himself let it be known that no favours could be expected from him. The only man who displayed, albeit cautiously, any sympathy for Christoff was the manager of the local mines. He liked music and on a number of occasions took Christoff to his home. Christoff often sang the songs of Rachmaninov, which he studied lovingly and whose excellence he rediscovered. In 1945, when he was released from the camp, he gave a Rachmaninov concert to the troops who liberated him. Afterwards, with the aid of the French camp commandant, an officer in the Foreign Legion, he returned to Rome and to Stracciari, but not without first experiencing difficulties.

At that time Rome was no longer at war, but the economy was bankrupt and much of the population lived in desperate poverty. Stracciari generously insisted that he would instruct his Bulgarian friend without payment. But Christoff did not even have enough money to buy food. The Italian admiral Roberti, who let him an apartment in his house and believed in his God-given gifts, did not ask for any money, while a card supplied by the Vatican qualified him for free food, although it was only once a day.

At this time, and for some years after, Christoff was officially stateless. As late as October 1956, the *New York*

*Times* commented: 'It has taken six years for the United States to issue a visa to Boris Christoff, the Bulgarian bass.' He has spoken little of these difficulties, for when a man has experienced success he may be reluctant to recall the bad times.

At the end of the war Stracciari was already 70 years old, but he continued to sing and to follow Christoff's development assiduously. His main concern was not to hurry him and to do everything methodically. Early in the summer of 1945 he was preparing to go on holiday. His pupil said to him in horror:

'Maestro, this is a disaster for me! Are we going to have a break?'

'Why not? I need a holiday and you can return to Bulgaria.'

'But that is by no means easy.'

'In that case, if everything is so tragic for you, come to Casalecchio. There you can sing with me and we can stay in the same house.'

The visit of the two friends to the beautiful little village of Casalecchio di Reno, near Bologna, was idyllic. They worked constantly, and Christoff became more and more convinced of how important this was for him. He knew how much his voice had benefited when Stracciari allowed him to sing the role of Ramphis in *Aïda*. More precisely, he understood for the first time the great significance of Verdi for the development, broadening and rounding out of the sonority of his voice. He understood that the past months in which he had only vocalized (without singing a single song) had not been in vain. Once, in the autumn of 1945, the two came into conflict: Stracciari wanted to discover how his pupil's voice sounded in a higher register, reaching up into the baritone range; and when Stracciari was surprised at its flexibility he tried to persuade Christoff to pitch higher. Christoff, however, objected, saying that he knew his own voice better. Giuseppe De Luca was called in as an arbiter. He said, 'Stracciari, give up this idea. Why should we make things difficult and torture a voice which is a natural bass?' At this the skies cleared and the co-operation continued successfully. And in 1945, after he had heard his pupil at his first recital in the Accademia di Santa Cecilia at Rome, Stracciari wrote on a photograph: 'To my beloved Boris, the future glory of Bulgaria.'

This significant début came about after he met Renato Fasano, director of Santa Cecilia and an influential figure in Italian music. Their meeting proved to have long-term consequences. Guido Sanpaoli, the future director of the Rome Opera, who had already heard and admired Christoff's artistry, was also present at this meeting. Fasano invited him to an audition. After Sanpaoli had heard him sing Boris Godunov's monologue he asked him if he would like to sign a contract for one concert right away or wait another year.

'Right away,' Christoff replied without hesitation.

'Can you sing Wotan's Farewell in Italian?'

'I can.'

The contract was signed that very evening, an evening Christoff will always remember. He recalls that he sang in front of an ancient picture of the Crucifixion hanging on the wall and that, when he had finished, Sanpaoli leapt from his chair and cried: 'Long live our leading singer! Long live Boris Christoff!' The storm of applause with which the audience responded may be considered to be the start of his triumphant professional career. That evening was the first of many similar meetings and contracts. Fasano invited Christoff to participate in every new season, and particularly to take part in Bach's *St Matthew Passion*, in which he performed for the first time under the baton of Otto Klemperer. Later he sang the work under Herbert von Karajan, most notably in a filmed performance that was shown frequently in the 1950s over Easter.

In the following years he was a travelling minstrel and became a member of the touring operatic company of Fausto De Tura. The public in the southern city of Reggio di Calabria, where the company was performing, greeted his début as Colline in Puccini's *La Bohème* with thunderous ovations, and he was obliged to sing Colline's Coat song, 'Vecchia zimarra', three times. After singing the small part of Cirillo in Giordano's *Fedora* at the Quirino theatre in Rome in 1946, he made his début in a major house as Pimen in Mussorgsky's *Boris Godunov* at the Rome Opera. The way was now open to La Scala.

Events now moved relatively quickly, owing in part to a kindly Italian lady, Signora Bolondi. This educated and intellectually curious woman lived in the same house in the Via Tre Madonne, near the Borghese Park, that had been inhabited by the admiral who had shown hospitality to Christoff. Christoff was still living in her apartment and had become friendly with her two sons, who were his contemporaries. One visitor to the house chanced to be Franca De Renzis, who was destined to become Christoff's wife. Christoff recalls that they first met on 15 March 1946. He had just returned from his first tour. Perhaps it was as a result of this day that his life became more complete. He remembers that Signora Bolondi whispered to him jokingly, 'That is the kind of wife you need.'

At this time Franca's father, Raffaelo De Renzis, had been dismissed from the *Il Giornale d'Italia*, despite his reputation as the most able Italian musicologist, because he had written a devastating review about the failings of a female singer who happened to have friends in high places. An air of high aesthetic taste pervaded his home. Well-known conductors such as Vittorio Gui and composers such as Umberto Giordano, Francesco Cilea and Wolf-Ferrari often visited the De Renzis home; the great Chaliapin had been a guest there. Franca's sister Tilde was a fine pianist. She used to accompany the pupils of the well-known tenor Giulio Crimi. It was at Crimi's house that she met Tito Gobbi, whom she later married. Franca, then, grew up surrounded by music. She followed the cultural life of the time with unusual pleasure and developed a finely tuned aesthetic taste. By the time Christoff came to know her she knew by heart every opera in the repertoire of the country's theatres. In this circle there was one other charming figure: Franca's mother, Signora Giuseppina, who came to adore Boris both as a singer and as a man and was a regular visitor to all his concerts and performances.

What Christoff received from the cultural and spiritual atmosphere of the house is impossible to quantify. He himself thinks that Raffaello De Renzis did not play a direct role in his artistic development, but he unquestionably derived benefit from access to De Renzis's enormous library, or more precisely that part of it which had not been donated to the Italian Institute of Music History in Rome, of which De Renzis was the head. His father-in-law would say to Boris, 'I am a nobleman, but penniless!'

'Father-in-law, blood is all the same. Nobility is to be discovered through the soul,' Christoff insisted.

That the De Renzis sisters should each marry a great singer was remarkable. In the early days, Gobbi felt he had to be in superlative form not to be put in the shade by Christoff's singing. In 1958 they were to sing together at Covent Garden in Verdi's *Don Carlos* (see Lord Harewood's Foreword). They also appeared together in *Nabucco*. And in the 1950s they recorded Verdi's *Simone Boccanegra*.

For Christoff, Franca was to be an inspirational companion. In October 1976 he dedicated the recording he had made in the Alexander Nevsky cathedral in Sofia to Franca with the following words: 'To Franca, my beloved wife and valued collaborator in the perfecting of my art, I dedicate my first performance on my native soil – the chants of our Orthodox Church for which she spontaneously conceived an affection.'

Since their marriage Christoff has scarcely ever travelled without Franca. She accompanied him to all the concert halls and opera houses which invited him to perform. Their devotion to each other is manifest to all – to their friends and to many conductors, orchestral players, and scene-shifters as well as to ordinary opera-goers all over the world. Franca was as perceptive and logical in her assessments and convictions about Boris's music as about their relationships with friends. She was, for him, the personification of family happiness, sitting beside him on a baroque sofa under a large painting of the ancient ruins by Panini. At the same time she was a demanding opera critic, and was quite capable of insisting that a rehearsal be brought to an end if it clearly was not going well.

At the recording sessions in the Alexander Nevsky cathedral in both 1976 and 1978, Christoff leaned on Franca for advice. She sat slightly to one side so as to be able to observe closely everyone and everything and in the breaks he would go up to her first of all and ask the same question each time: 'How was it?' All the notes of the producer, conductor and sound recordists were checked in conversations with her, or were completely changed as a result of her assessment. Nobody was surprised by this because it appeared natural, and everyone felt that it was necessary and correct. That is how it was in the Bulgaria Hall at the end of November 1977 at the first recording of the Grechaninov songs. At this time Christoff's work can be likened to that of an engraver trying to find the completed drawing on the copper surface. At some points on the 'drawing' he had to tighten up and emphasize; at others he had to sound ethereal. Whenever it was a question of such nuances, he turned to Franca.

Some critics have been worried by Franca's dominant participation in rehearsals. But her influence was so integral to the development of the style of Christoff's magnificent talent that there is little point in criticizing it. Perhaps that is why, after arduous rehearsals or prolonged applause, the two of them often prefer to go off by themselves. In Copenhagen in 1977 a special room was prepared for them to which they could steal away from the Tivoli concert hall. One might say, 'They're just like schoolchildren!' And why not? Did not Boris Christoff himself say that one has to study until the end of one's life?

Of course, there was hardship. Perhaps only Franca could say how much stress there was before the rounds of applause. Her husband has a strong character and does not easily suppress his own natural instincts. When a journalist from *Il Tempo* asked her what she thought of him, she replied as follows: 'My husband is a tough customer. But he is an exceptional and highly cultured man. He speaks and writes six languages, he is a keen bibliophile and he collects antiques from all over the world. Just like Henry VIII, whom he played at the Teatro dell'Opera, he should have six wives: he is very pernickety. His greatest quality? He envies no one and hates no one, despite the hostility and attacks from people of absolutely no quality. His greatest failing? He is totally preoccupied and not aware of his surroundings. Also ... he is not very sociable: he does not make friends with the authorities. He does not know how to, and does not wish to, develop those connections that for some are essential in the mysterious world of the opera. In general, after living for decades in Italy, Boris is still treated as a foreigner. As a result he prefers to travel to America, Germany or Britain, countries that have the greatest respect for him.'

In the immediate post-war years, Christoff met a number of outstanding people who made a lasting impact on his life. He found these people because he needed them. He was truly fortunate that they were at the height of their creative powers at the time and were generous in dispensing their knowledge of the lasting achievements of the creative impulse. In Trieste he got to know the great actor and producer Alexander Akimovich Sanin (1869–1956). Those who are aware of Sanin's fruitful co-operation with Stanislavsky at the Moscow Art Theatre, his production of *Boris Godunov* in Paris in 1908, and the careers of his pupils, who included Chaliapin, can appreciate the significance of the acquaintanceship, especially when it was so enthusiastically sought by both parties. At the time Sanin was producing Mussorgsky's *Khovanshchina* at the Trieste Opera. Christoff wanted to learn from him something that he considered essential to interpret correctly every other opera: to learn how to portray the tragic tsar, Boris Godunov, and how to achieve the correct gestures and detail. As rarely happens, fate was helpful. Not long afterwards Christoff sang in productions of *Boris Godunov* by Sanin in Cagliari and Rome.

Similarly Christoff got to know the conductor Issay Dobrowen (1894–1953). This marvellous man and artist had followed Christoff's development with a benevolent eye since his first concerts at the Santa Cecilia, but at first he had kept his distance. Then in 1949 he approached Boris and suggested: 'I think that you must sing with me in *Khovanshchina*.' After that the friendship between the two became true and lasting. Occasionally they would test one another, grow impatient or quarrel, but they knew that they would continue to work together, united as they were by common beliefs. After Trieste and Venice, Christoff was playing in his third production of *Khovanshchina* but despite all the experience that had been gathered, Dobrowen suggested 'a special rehearsal' for him. That was not because he had doubts about Christoff's performance but because he respected him. His ideas and suggestions on this occasion were an expression of unshakeable confidence. Later, in 1951–2, they quarrelled over Christoff's doubling the roles of Galitsky and Konchak in Borodin's *Prince Igor*, and this time Dobrowen won the argument: Christoff sang just one part.

# 3

## Recognition

Recognition arrived relatively quickly. Only a few months had elapsed since the former prisoner had returned to Rome to live on a card providing free food supplied by the Vatican when the doors to creative happiness opened up for him. In December 1945, when he appeared before the Italian public for the first time in a recital, the Rome press noted: 'We must thank the Santa Cecilia for giving us the opportunity to hear for the first time in Rome the bass Boris Christoff ... who sang, in the original, several beautiful Bulgarian and Russian songs with very fine taste.... He showed that not only does he have a beautiful and well-trained voice but also that he is an excellent artist who is fully mature despite his youth. He is a singer that we should like to hear in opera.'

As we have seen, this wish was fulfilled in September 1946. After his magnificent performance in the role of Colline in Puccini's *La Bohème* in the city of Reggio di

Calabria, he appeared at theatres in the major Italian cities and by 1948 he had prepared or performed more than 10 major roles. Opera-lovers had heard him as Ramphis in *Aïda*, Oroveso in *Norma*, Dosifey in *Khovanshchina*, and Pimen in *Boris Godunov*. He had appeared at the Rome Opera, at San Carlo in Naples, in the summer season at the Caracalla Baths in Rome and at the Trieste Opera. In 1949 the doors of La Scala were opened for him. In one season alone there he sang Dosifey in *Khovanshchina*, Count Robinson in Cimarosa's *Il matrimonio segreto* and Galitsky and Konchak in *Prince Igor*. In 1950 he was invited to the Maggio Musicale in Florence, where on 27 May he sang Philip II in Verdi's *Don Carlos*.

All these triumphs owed much to Christoff's studies with Stracciari and his contacts with Sanin, Labinski and Dobrowen, as well as to his own powerful talent. In the years that followed the people of Rome looked upon his successes as their own. The local papers carried lengthy reviews not only of his appearances at the Rome Opera and at La Scala but also of his tours of New York, San Francisco, London and Paris on 18 April 1954 *Il Tempo* wrote of the first night of Gluck's *Iphigénie en Aulide* at the Teatro del Opera in Rome: 'As always, Christoff gave a colossal performance. It is not easy to find on the operatic stage a more convincing balance between the spirit of the classics and the intensity of stress than in Christoff's performance in the role of Agamemnon.' Four years later the same paper wrote again, about his assumption of the title role in Rossini's opera *Mosè*: 'One performer who displayed an astonishingly musical and psychological insight was the bass Boris Christoff ... With great mastery he embodied the monumental figure of Moses, taking him down from his pedestal and, with the aid of the music, making of him a living being.'

At Florence's Maggio Musicale as early as 1951, he took the

role of the rebel Procida in *I Vespri siciliani*, with Maria Callas as Elena, under the baton of Kleiber (see Discography). Christoff set a high standard and afterwards his participation at this festival was the most reliable guarantee that these standards would be maintained: three decades later the organizers of the festival were continuing to invite him to take part. Many reviews refer to his performances in the summer seasons in Rome at the open-air theatre at the Baths of Caracalla. Critics wrote most admiringly about his part in arousing interest in Russian music, and several reviewers wrote perceptively of Christoff's ability to unite the beauty of Italian legato with the rich nuances of Slavonic sensibility.

Some two decades later, in 1977, the journalist Enrico Cavalotti quoted these words of Christoff: 'In recent years interest in the musical theatre has fallen to a worrying level. The leaders in this sphere are largely responsible for this – the administrators and artistic directors, most of whom are incapable of carrying out their duties because they are incompetent.... Nowadays everyone seems to be carried away by an irresistible attraction to "historic discoveries", but many operas are performed without standards by producers who are in thrall to frivolous impresarios, to singers who are not prepared and are incapable of performing the roles they have to play....' Cavalotti published these views under the headline: 'A meeting with the Bulgarian bass Christoff.' They were seen as the conclusions of a man who had been linked by fate with contemporary Italian musical culture, and who was expressing the sorrow of an artist whose achievements in opera houses all over the world guaranteed that his opinions would be respected.

These achievements were mentioned in a sincere and colourful manner by the well-known Italian tenor, Giacomo Lauri-Volpi, who at the end of his career gave his views on all the noteworthy artists with whom he had sung in the opera-house or whom he had heard sing. In his interesting book *Voci Parallele*, published in 1977, he has a section entitled 'Voci di basso' in which he juxtaposed Chaliapin and Rossi-Lemeni, Gaudio and Pasero, Mardones and Neri, De Angelis and Journet, Pinza and Siepi, and Chirino and Reuter. In this section he draws a parallel between Boris Christoff and the Polish bass Adam Didur: 'Nature gave Didur a voice with a great range in the high notes and voluminous in the low notes. It gave him an athletic body and an expressive face.... But all this was not accompanied by the technical means of expression. In a short time he had used up all his capital.... At the Metropolitan he hid his glorious voice behind a walk-on artist.... It is one of the most pitiful sights one can see when an artist appearing on the stage has a voice which begins to stutter in agony as if he were sick with fear.... If Didur had done as Christoff had done and used his voice intelligently he would have retained his powers longer and he would not have been tormented by daily tribulations. The Bulgarian has discovered a guiding thread and keeps to it as a train keeps to the rails. He knows the physical limits of his singing and this gives him a great advantage. Didur explodes the notes while Christoff sings them in order to link, weld and embellish them, always alert and aware of the limits of his vocal powers. He has used his intellectual gifts to occupy a worthy place on the operatic stage. In this he had the benefit of a noble collaboration with Riccardo Stracciari, his predecessor.'

This view of Christoff's greatness was shared not only by the critics and contemporary operatic stars but also by thousands of Italian music-lovers. In 1975 the managing committee of the Association of the Friends of the Teatro Reggio in Turin awarded prizes for three consecutive years

(1972–5) to 'two singers, born in Bulgaria and trained in Italy, Boris Christoff and Raina Kabaivanska'. They considered the two singers had made a lasting impression not only on the process of cultural rapprochement between Italy and Bulgaria but on efforts to enrich the musical life of our time. Shortly afterwards, in 1977, when the Bulgarian government awarded Boris Christoff the title of People's Artist, the Friends of the Teatro Reggio sent Christoff a telegram: 'The creator of a unique link between the Slavonic race and the Italian school, in your brilliant thirty-year career you have, by means of the intellectual influence of your particularly inimitable vocal timbre, your supernatural gifts and profound interpretations, given the world an example of a rare personality with vocal and acting gifts, inspired by a general predisposition towards a proud and tormented mastery that is never divorced from a profound and inextinguishable feeling of humanity.'

Against this background, the concert which Christoff gave on 18 February 1977 in the concert hall of Santa Cecilia, in the same institute in which his rise to fame began in December 1946, is particularly significant. The posters and programmes described the concert as an anniversary event, but the press treated it as a celebration. It demonstrated his great mastery of vocalization, his ability to colour every syllable and sound and to underline the variation in phrasing. Those in the hall followed him as if they had been enchanted. He performed for them the forgotten musical heritage of the Italian *seicento* and *settecento* as well as magnificent pages from the works of Schubert and the songs of Rachmaninov and Rimsky-Korsakov. When he bowed after the last song everyone present in the hall rose, and cries of 'bravo!' could be heard from all sides. As an encore, Christoff performed two more songs, one by Mussorgsky and the other a Russian folk-song. These seemed to increase the enthusiasm.

Reviewing the concert under the heading 'Boris Christoff celebrates thirty years of performing in Rome', *Unità*'s critic noted that the singer who had given magnificent performances of the great roles of the operatic stage had now displayed a noteworthy 'style, nobility and exceptional intelligence'. *Il Popolo*'s reviewer wrote that the concert was 'another of the successes that this renowned Bulgarian bass (but one may also add "Italian", since the greater part of his artistic career has been spent in our country) has achieved in all the major opera houses in the world.'

Christoff's lightning success in Rome and Milan quickly resounded beyond the frontiers of Italy. This marked the beginning of his triumphs in all the great opera-houses of the world. His first recordings would spread his fame to those distant places where he had not yet appeared.

Critics wrote of his tours in the most enthusiastic terms. On 1 October 1956, the *New York Times* insisted that Boris Christoff 'had to be compared with the legendary Russian Feodor Chaliapin'. Two years later, on 18 November 1958, the *Chicago Daily News* wrote that he was 'a genius of the lyric theatre, whose portrait of the Tsar tormented by pangs of conscience is on a par with those of Chaliapin, Kipnis and Pinza. This is a Boris that deserves to be described by historians and that will remain a legend.'

From this time forward the crown of supremacy seemed to have been awarded to him for good. Critics rarely resorted to comparisons and did so only to dub him 'the tsar of basses', 'great' or 'incomparable'. In 1971 *The Times* wrote of Christoff's performances in *Khovanshchina* and *Mosè* at the Rome Opera in terms scarcely less detailed or enthusiastic than those of the Italian press. On 1 July 1956, in connection with his début in Buenos Aires, the Argentinian press wrote of him as an artist who had already been recognized and who had created 'portraits which belong to an entire generation'. London regretted that it had not seen all the roles for which he was renowned. On 18 October 1973, the *Daily Telegraph* highly praised his Fiesco in Verdi's *Simone Boccanegra* and insisted: 'Mr Christoff must return soon and delight us with his other roles.'

At the beginning of the 1950s Christoff had also become popular in France. Parisian musical circles knew about him before his triumphant appearance at the Opéra. To be more precise, they already appreciated him and awaited with growing impatience the moment when he would be seen among them. Records had played a significant role in advancing his reputation, and it was in France in 1953 that he received the first important award for them: an international gramophone award for his performances of three roles in *Boris Godunov*: Pimen, Varlaam and Boris. As if to underline this award still more emphatically, there were others outside the official prize-giving.

In the same year, 1953, he seems to have exceeded the expectations of even his staunchest admirers in Paris. Of his performance as Boris Godunov, the *Figaro* correspondent Clarendon wrote: 'In the Kremlin scene a miracle occurred.... He played the role with such dramatic force and such vocal riches that the audience applauded him ceaselessly. But that was nothing compared with the Death, where this great artist gave us a lesson in terror the like of which I have never seen in the theatre and which I cannot describe.... Truly this is a miracle of intensity, nobility and emotion.' *Combat* was also entranced: 'The voice of Boris Christoff glows with noble power, with delicacy and breadth which conceal a fully developed technique.... In comparison with the voice of his renowned predecessor [Chaliapin] the voice of Christoff appears to be more rounded, softer and not so "blaring", with an approach which is more Italian than Slavonic. His *pianissimo* never affects the quality of the timbre and his rich voice is imbued with moving flexibility. All this is a matter of true wonder.'

Such singing – and such enthusiastic response to it – is exceedingly rare. But Christoff seems to have repeated this triumph when he returned to the Paris Opéra in 1966. The critic of *Les Arts* wrote: 'Boris Christoff's return to Paris was eagerly anticipated. It is known that Boris Christoff stopped singing for more than a year because of a serious illness. Last December [1965] he appeared again, in *Boris Godunov* in London. Afterwards in *Julius Caesar* in Venice.... His voice sounded broader and more beautiful than it had ever been. His timbre in two octaves, as good in the *pianissimo* as it is in the *forte*, is a real miracle. His vocal art is incomparable: the manner in which Christoff understands and feels the music, the legato with which he supports the musical phrases, and finally the great sense of tragedy which is revealed during his interpretations....' In 1983, the French critics were as enthusiastic as of old. As the critic in *La Lettre Française* wrote: 'Boris Christoff is staggering. One cannot dream of a more complete interpretation. It is a moment of revelation: the farewell to his son, the Tsarevich, and the death of Boris touch you to the depths of your heart.... In fact, it is not theatre, it is not opera, it is no kind of convention.... it is a moment of agony, of death.... His voice is again warm, velvety and noble, his acting comes from the heart and is illuminated by the intellect.... Boris Christoff remains the most magnificent bass of our time.'

Also in 1983 the monthly journal *Diapason* had written

of one of his recitals: 'The first joy is surprise. The enormous, beautiful voice is untouched and unchanged by age (he is over 60), his sonority in pianissimo is complete and at the fortissimo it is unshakeably secure and absolutely smooth in all registers. Is this a miracle of nature, of faultless technique or of the knowledge and wisdom of the performer? Perhaps it is a combination of all of these things.

'The second joy is a rare experience – an encounter with a school which is practically unknown today, the school of the purest bel canto. It enables one to achieve everything in the entire repertoire: nuances of style, lightness in the production of the voice known as "line": a sign of nobility in singing by which, before Bellini, one recognized the gods.

'The third joy is the presence. From his appearance on the stage up to the final applause, from his gestures to his gaze, and every moment of a strictly stylish and difficult programme (Mussorgsky in the first part, Mussorgsky in the second and Mussorgsky as an encore), there was an unbelievable presence of a personality, of a temperament. This can neither be discussed nor understood. It simply exists and we bow before it.

'On 22 November 1982, an individual appeared before an enthusiastic and enchanted public who in ancient times would have been described as a demi-god. How else can we describe one of the greatest singers of the 20th century? When the concert was over we were obliged to return to earth, to the present day, and our senses were overflowing with a sense of something incredible....'

At the end of 1949, Boris Christoff was invited to Britain to take the title role in *Boris Godunov*. The invitation arose as a result of the early records (see Discography) he had made with Dobrowen. His self-confidence had grown to such an extent that he was in no hurry to agree to all the conditions, and disagreements arose between him and the management of Covent Garden. One area of disagreement was particularly important: which of the two versions of *Boris Godunov* was to be performed – the original Mussorgsky or the Rimsky-Korsakov version? His desire to triumph at this famous opera house was strong, but his sense of independence was even greater. Covent Garden was then performing the Mussorgsky; Christoff preferred the Rimsky. The administrator of the Royal Opera House, David Webster, proposed a compromise: Christoff should sing his version of his part; the rest should be performed as normal.

This seemed to settle matters – but then a new problem arose. Shortly before the opening, and after he had sung at a rehearsal without sets, Christoff saw something on stage which puzzled him. In Peter Brook's controversial staging, in the Prologue there were stakes with bells attached to them, an enormous clock upstage in the Clock scene, and finally dozens of knives dripping blood which descended from the skies in the Hallucination scene. Christoff considered all this frivolous, even sacrilegious. In his view one could do that sort of thing in modern works, but one should not tamper with the classics.

He went to the designer and producer and told them indignantly that he was dismayed. He pointed out that in the first act there was an enormous terrace and he could not see how he was to appear on it. Of course the producer had his own ideas, explaining that there would be a step ladder, that at first only his head would be visible and later the rest of his body. The young Peter Brook was at that time noted for his productions of Shakespeare. This *Boris Godunov* was his first contact with opera and Christoff was not inclined to trust him. From his studies with Sanin he knew that the entrance of Tsar Boris should fill everyone on stage with terror, and he told Brook, 'I am not a performing animal.' Brook could not accept Christoff's objections. Christoff then went to Webster. He was alarmed not only because of the horrors on stage but also because of their effect on the development of modern opera. His quarrel with Brook had to do with the classic dilemma facing artists of divergent views: whether radically 'contemporary' interpretations of classic works undermine the integrity of such works; and whether an insistence upon 'traditional' interpretations eventually loses the power to move modern audiences.

When matters were delayed still further, Christoff announced that he would pay for not fulfilling his contract and was planning to leave. Outside the opera house, he and Franca met Herbert von Karajan, who had heard about the dispute and who now advised him not to be too hasty; after all, Covent Garden was very important to him. For Christoff, however, there was no room for compromise. He spent several hours behind closed doors at his hotel, ready at any moment to leave for Italy without money and without acclaim but with the feeling that he had preserved his independence. Everyone appeared at loggerheads. Then, on the evening before their intended departure, the telephone rang. It was David Webster, who said: 'Forget everything that has happened; please come back.' After that all went smoothly. Although there were only a few hours before the opening, all the changes he requested were carried out. In the final act the throne was raised seven or eight steps. Since there was little time for alterations, the shortcomings in the set were concealed by lighting.

After the evening's success the unpleasant exchanges were forgotten. The portrait of Boris created by Christoff overwhelmed all reservations, and gave pleasure to all. There would be other disagreements in his subsequent engagements at Covent Garden, but by then mutual trust and respect allowed matters to be settled quickly and amicably. Over the years the British critics have not spared their praise. In addition to his portrayals of Boris Godunov and Philip II, that of Fiesco in *Simone Boccanegra*, the third role that Christoff has played at Covent Garden, has also been acclaimed..

Later, when the British press began to realize that Christoff was singing on the British stage for the fourth decade and had begun to describe him as a veteran, the experts nonetheless continued to expect something new from him. They expressed interest in his wish to include in his London repertoire the title roles in Massenet's *Don Quichotte* and Glinka's *A Life for the Tsar*, or Khan Konchak in *Prince Igor*. Their regrets that these never took place were sincere since he continued to impress them with examples of his great talent. On 1 November 1974, the *Daily Express* wrote: 'Exactly 25 years ago the Bulgarian-born singer sang the leading role in *Boris Godunov* on this stage for the first time. This same singer, then unknown, began his rise to world fame from here. Then thanks to his portrayal and his outstanding qualities this opera was able to put down roots on the British stage, opening the ears of a new generation to Russian national opera.' These lines, even by themselves, are enough to justify a creative life. It is a question of the inspiration of a whole generation, and such recognition is accorded to few artists while they are still alive.

The reviews of the concerts and performances which Christoff gave in England in 1973 and 1974 are particularly favourable. On 7 September 1974, Robert Henderson wrote in the *Daily Telegraph*: 'Boris Christoff made one of his very rare appearances in the concert halls of our country. Last night he gave a solo performance at a Promenade Concert in the Albert Hall with the orchestra of the Royal Opera House under Colin Davis. The effect he had on the audience with his performance of the two great death scenes in Russian opera, Glinka's *A Life for the Tsar* and Mussorgsky's *Boris Godunov*, was magnificent and enchanting examples of his unusual and typical timbre – a quality which can only belong to the great actor-singers. Without the help of scenic effects and costumes and with the minimum of gesture, he was able to create a convincing and powerful illusion of a character and a condition simply by means of one subtle and scarcely perceptible vocal inflection.'

Another critic spoke of the same concert on BBC Radio Three in these terms: 'Boris Christoff died twice in last night's Prom at the Albert Hall, but in the noblest meaning of the phrase. I am referring to the two scenes from Russian grand opera: *A Life for the Tsar* and, of course, the death scene from *Boris Godunov*. His voice is in excellent form. I doubt if any other bass in the world at present can attract so effortlessly such an audience to the Albert Hall as he did last night. Is there any other bass in the world whose tone is so concentrated and so well focused on the centre of the note without any sense of strain? ... His voice with its regal dying tone soared above the chorus of Polish soldiers (the BBC Singers). He performed Ivan Susanin's farewell to life in a melancholy tone, as black as coal, at the same time retaining the clear, pure brilliance of his voice. Christoff achieves expression in his voice in the best possible manner – from the sound and meaning of the words that he sings. When he sings these terrifying and tormented sounds and syllables in Russian and they emerge from his enormous throat, the effect is fantastic.'

A review in *The Times* of 2 June 1973 of a Christoff

concert was just as enthusiastic: 'Scarcely had the triumph of his Dosifey at Florence died down than Boris Christoff came to the Maltings, Snape, for one of his rare appearances in a recital. For the occasion he assembled a programme consisting only of songs by Mussorgsky, based on the cycles *Sunless* and *Songs and Dances of Death*, but these songs with their rather sombre colouring suited Christoff's expressive voice to perfection – he possesses a wide range despite the fact that his timbre is that of a bass – and his voice was in excellent form.' In the *Daily Express* of 1 November 1974, Noel Goodwin wrote: 'Boris Christoff, one of the greatest basses in the world, celebrated his special anniversary with his return to one of Russia's greatest musical works, which was performed last night at Covent Garden.... On this occasion Mr Christoff displayed the same excellence on the stage as the Tsar as he always has.... In places in the "nightmare" scene his acting was perhaps a little extravagant, but his singing was excellent – and as always he helped the other singers on the enormous stage to give of their best.'

In *Opera* (November 1974), the 25th anniversary of Christoff's Covent Garden début was marked by a feature showing photos of him in all his major roles. The 30th anniversary of his Royal Opera début was celebrated by an exhibition consisting of photographs of him in various roles and a variety of episodes from his life: Boris when little, Boris with his wife Franca, Boris on the stages of the great opera houses of the world. The exhibition covered his personal experiences and enthusiasms. The centrepiece was a full-length portrait by Leonard Boden of Christoff in the role of Boris Godunov (see over), in which he had begun his triumphs at Covent Garden in 1949. That evening, at a Prom performance in the house Christoff sang the role of King

Philip II. He seemed uplifted by the accumulated glory and wisdom of past years, and the audience felt the drama of the work as if they were experiencing it for the first time. When the performance ended the auditorium exploded in a storm of shouts and applause. The seats of the stalls had been taken out, and the audience sat or stood on the floor: a different audience, younger and more attentive, from that which usually occupies the lowest level of the house. They fell silent when the Covent Garden general director, Sir John Tooley, appeared at one side of the stage. He held in his hand a small box containing a special medal in honour of Christoff's distinguished services to music, and said a few words about Christoff's many years of creative association with Covent Garden. Christoff replied briefly in English; and later, still in his make-up, he showed his medal to the television cameras.

Christoff's fame also preceded him to the United States. In 1949, the impresario Sol Hurok invited him to make a tour with Herbert von Karajan and Victor De Sabata. Unfortunately at that time the knights of the Cold War often suspected artists from Eastern Europe of being agents in disguise. The Bulgarian bass was refused an entry visa as an 'undesirable visitor because of his contacts with the Russians and as a Bulgarian subject'. However, his inextinguishable talent could not be denied, and Christoff developed many personal contacts with music lovers in America.

More than 20 years later American newspapers would recall his denial of an entry visa with regret. On 25 March 1980 the *New York Times* wrote: 'Mr Christoff, one of the greatest basses and singer-actors, should have made his début at the Metropolitan in the role of King Philip in Verdi's *Don Carlos* as long ago as 1950, in the first season of

Rudolf Bing's directorship. However, this coincided with the height of the McCarthyite hysteria and Mr Christoff, a Bulgarian, was refused a visa by the government. For many reasons, most of which were groundless, he has never sung at the Metropolitan, and in fact before this evening he had sung only once before in New York....' On the same day Harriet Johnson declared on the pages of the *New York Post*: 'In 1950, when Senator McCarthy's witch-hunt was on the prowl for so-called Communists, Christoff was refused permission to take part in the first performance of a new production of *Don Carlos* at the Metropolitan because he had a Bulgarian passport, despite the fact that he had been living in Italy for six years and had never been a member of any political party.'

Christoff had made his United States début in San Francisco in September 1956. He was greeted with acclaim. On 27 September 1956, the *San Francisco Examiner* rated his arrival as a major event and presented him to its readers as 'a magnetic central figure in a scenically new production – which is really beautifully conceived. Christoff's finest contribution is the exceptional beauty of his voice. It is a great quality in the role which truly corresponds to a Russian Richard III.... Boris Christoff's voice fully resembles that of Chaliapin – rich, mellow and with Slavonic overtones and finesse.' In the *Oakland Tribune* Clifford Gessler wrote that Christoff had been received enthusiastically 'by the packed auditorium of the War Memorial Opera House' and that his voice had qualities and a range that made it unusual. On 1 October 1956 the *New York Times* wrote: 'This creation of Boris Christoff is worthy of comparison with the performances of the legendary Russian, Feodor Chaliapin. Mr Christoff presented a tempest of emotions. When he is on stage the opera begins to assume an unexpected dimension. It is transformed into the core and essence of life.'

In March 1980 these quotations were recalled and re-emphasized. One of the American reviewers, Bill Zakariasen, wrote: '... Assisted by the generally good chorus and orchestra of the Musical Society under Angelo Campori, Christoff sang arias from Verdi's operas *Macbeth* and *Don Carlos*, in which his interpretation of "Ella giammai m'amò" has become a classic, with a great sense of tragedy and without a trace of self-pity. Boris's farewell and death from *Boris Godunov* by Mussorgsky were once again performed magnificently and the scarcely audible *pianissimi* were capable of inspiring the fear of God in any other contemporary bass. The "Songs and Dances of Death" were the most beautiful – four miniatures of musical drama whose rendition was permeated with terror and romanticism.' And Zakariasen concluded: 'The colossi still among us are rather few.'

In his review Byron Belt noted: 'At just over sixty years old, Christoff's bass remains a unique instrument. It can melt with black anger but it can also be transformed into the most exquisite *mezza voce* that we have heard from any modern singer. The power and perfection of his art is so exceptional that merely to see and hear him is a lesson in musical communication.... After an unusually warm reception the concert began rather poorly. Campori led into Banquo's aria from *Macbeth* with the improbable introduction to this chaotic opera. When Christoff began he seemed to be frozen with nerves and his performance served no other purpose than to allow him to relax amid the warmth of his admiring public.... But the first half ended with a stunning choral performance of Verdi's *Stabat Mater* and afterwards perhaps the greatest bass scene in Italian opera:

"Ella giammai m'amò" from *Don Carlos*.... The artist reproduced the profound melancholy and despair of the betrayed monarch better than ever before.... One was almost unprepared for the fact that a singer in a white tie and tails could so comprehensively master every nuance and that one could sense once again the presence of true grandeur. Glory!'

Harriet Johnson's review in the *New York Post* of 25 March 1980 was equally enthusiastic. 'With a handsome figure, although he is over sixty, and a steady step and a frightening, even evil gaze, the bass took the stage with an elegance which was suitable for a film on the theme of prosperity; a retired spy and the most aristocratic secret agent of Scotland Yard. In the beginning his voice, which is a more brilliant and resonant bass than the darker Chaliapin type, was drier as a result of an easily understandable nervousness. His stage performance embodied all the terrible and dark deeds of which he sang. But the ice melted, although the singer had not yet smiled, when he came to Mussorgsky and he began to feel the Russian tongue and music which is clearly in the blood of a Slav. He performed some parts of Boris's farewell and death much more slowly than he would have been allowed to do in a performance of the whole opera, but it sounded convincing. There was so much heartrending pathos in his performance that when he sang "My Sister, protect my children", the audience felt that he was dying with every sound.'

The review of Donal Henahan in the *New York Times* was shaped by his recollections of Christoff's performances on earlier occasions: 'Boris Christoff is the finest King Philip of our time and this is revealed in the touching monologue "Ella giammai m'amò".... His voice sounds absolutely clear, at the disposal of one of the most powerful and expressive artists we have heard live.... It was as if we had gone back more than twenty years in time and were having this same experience for the first time. At that time some of us were not affected by the idiotic restrictions in casting at the Metropolitan and were able to hear Boris Christoff's complete repertoire in other, luckier cities.... It is true that his hair has turned grey and his thunderous voice has perhaps decreased by one or two decibels on certain notes. Nevertheless, that Christoff who once enchanted Carnegie Hall is still a great artist whose presence does honour to any opera house in the world. His *piano* singing was not technically accomplished but the sound was surprisingly good and his thunderous tones were to be found everywhere as the situation required. After so many years, bravo for Boris!'

In the second half of the 1950s Christoff's travels took him to South America. Musical circles there knew quite a lot about him and the applause in the opera houses showed that he had confirmed their happiest expectations. On 1 August 1956, *Buenos Aires Musical* wrote: 'A Boris such as that of Christoff – and of this there is absolutely no doubt – is a Boris for an entire generation. Majestic with a regal bearing such as the ruler of all the Russias should have in the Coronation scene, and his voice and accent in the monologue "My soul is suffering", create a bitterness that alarms one, a sincerity that touches one, and a depth that wrings one's heart. In the great scene in the Tsar's chambers in the second act his interpretation succeeds in making us forget our surroundings because his artistic personality is so absorbing when he portrays the fate of the hero. We see before us a suffering human being, a man spiritually broken with remorse. Christoff's acting in the pathetic death scene was a logical continuation of everything that had preceded it. His portrayal of the dying Tsar contains stern majesty, a noble quality, an impressiveness and a human eloquence. The curtain comes down, and to some extent the death of Boris Godunov is our own death because Christoff's spiritual palette has revealed to us the most intimate aspects of the Tsar and enabled us to penetrate into the darkest labyrinths of his soul. Moreover, after we have heard his Boris we are able fully to appreciate the words of Mussorgsky: "When I composed Boris, I felt that I was Boris." We, too, can do this thanks to the magic of a great artist.' During the same tour the newspaper *Diurnal* wrote on 2 August 1956 that in *The Barber of Seville* Boris Christoff as Don Basilio had exceeded 'all others with his gigantic stature as a singer' and had raised himself to an almost Biblical grandeur.

In the 1950s Christoff made a third tour of Spain. He sang only at the Liceo in Barcelona but his performances in *Boris Godunov* are still remembered throughout the country. He himself recalls that the performances were tiring because they began at 10 o'clock in the evening and ended at 3 in the morning, which fits in with the daily routine of the modern Spaniard but is unusual for a foreigner. In the long interval every member of the audience went down to the restaurant on the lower floor, and this locally traditional custom can also disturb the routine of a performer. But those who judge things from a professional point of view remember these performances for other things: for their artistic richness, their atmosphere and for the appeal of Christoff as a unique phenomenon. During these performances he tried for the first time the experiment of having the entire cast sing in Russian. Even a visiting German female singer sang in Russian. He brought with him other Bulgarian singers, among them the tenor Todor Mazarov, who sang the role of Dmitri the Pretender.

*Top, left:* The young Boris Christoff on his fourth birthday. *Top, right:* with his wife Franca, en route for New York. *Bottom:* Boris and Franca holidaying at Montecatini Terme, Italy, 1960.

As Boris Godunov at Covent Garden, 1949. (*Opera*)

As Dosifey in Mussorgsky's *Khovanshchina*, La Scala, 1949. (*Opera*)

As Galitsky in Borodin's *Prince Igor*, La Scala, 1951. (*Opera*)

As Konchak in *Prince Igor*, Chicago, 1962. (*Nancy Sorenson, Lyric Opera of Chicago*)

In 1976, as if in compensation for having waited so long, music lovers in Madrid awarded Christoff an ovation which could only be described as sensational. The local press described his performance in *Don Carlos* at the XIII Opera Festival as an 'Apotheosis'. On 22 April 1976, the newspaper *ABC* wrote: 'A star-studded cast. Voices of the very highest quality. The voice of Boris Christoff in the role of Philip II overcomes any worries that may arise because of age, thanks to his exceptionally high skills. There is a wealth of nuance – from the sternest severity to the tenderness of the love lament – so far as acting is concerned, his gestures, costume and the way in which he imposes his presence, in which he acts, speaks and even the way in which he acknowledges the applause, which was spontaneous and lasted several minutes.'

One of the European cities in which Christoff was greeted with enthusiastic and seemingly endless ovations was Copenhagen. His star rose there in 1967; it has never set since that time. In February 1967 he visited Copenhagen with the Bologna opera company to take part in a festival of Italian opera which was dominated by his presence. He was called by one critic 'the lyrical genius of our age'. In his review of 18 February 1967 in *Politiken*, Robert Naur wrote: 'It is true that the Royal Opera is not La Scala and that the Falconer Centre is not the Lincoln Center, but for Danish opera-lovers it is not without significance that in the course of one year they have been able to hear an artist like Boris Christoff in two of his greatest interpretations, first of all as Boris in *Boris Godunov* and on Thursday as King Philip.... They, the public, know very well that they have encountered Europe's operatic art since they filled the theatre and since they greeted Boris Christoff with applause that echoed in the auditorium for a long time.' Naur concluded that Christoff possessed a bass of unforgettable beauty and that he belonged to the highest rank in the musical world.

In *Information* of 17 February 1967, H. Lentz wrote that when Christoff came on stage it at once became clear how few other people there were who were blessed with a beautiful voice: 'All those around him in the opera were merely puppets'. He went on: 'The performance of *Don Carlos* during the festival of Italian opera had something which was lacking from the performance of *Rigoletto*: a single authentic artistic personality in the cast. We have once again had the opportunity to admire Boris Christoff.... In the role of Philip he becomes a true symbol of great art.... Even when Christoff turns his back to the audience we are struck dumb by his powerful talent.'

On one occasion the Danish royal family attended a performance of *Boris Godunov*. Christoff was told that if, at the end of the performance, there was a silver fanfare and the monarch stood up, the first bow must be to him. In practice, it turned out quite differently. After the silver fanfare there was a call from the whole orchestra, but when Christoff turned he saw that, as well as the king, the entire audience was on its feet. He did not know to whom to bow first: thousands of eyes glittering with happiness were turned towards him. In the event, the first bow was directed to them, the thousands of people who had been enraptured by his performance. Protocol was forgotten.

Critics and audiences were equally enthusiastic about Christoff's appearances at Salzburg and Vienna. The response of the demanding Austrian public to his performances did not waver over four decades. So far as earlier appearances are concerned it is sufficient to quote the reaction of the critic Karl Löbl to his appearance at the

1962 Salzburg Festival: 'Only Boris Christoff possesses the true and full range of quality as a singer and actor which is required for such a celebration at Salzburg. The opera *Don Carlos* should be called "Philip II" when this role is performed by Boris Christoff.... His voice glows both with the power of its range as well as with its warmth, its true profundity and nobility and its exceptionally beautiful pianissimo.... It is an example of refined phrasing and cultured vocal sensitivity.' The special correspondent of *Sovietskaya Muzika* in Salzburg, the musicologist I. Nestev, wrote of the same performances: 'The central figure in *Don Carlos* was the Slav, Boris Christoff, the well-known Bulgarian bass who was playing Philip II. His voice is noteworthy for its enormous power, the wealth of nuances is astounding – from the thunderous angry outbursts to the most delicate *pianissimo*. His acting reaches the height of dramatic art in the true sense of the words.'

# 4

## *Christoff and Operatic Character*

In the second half of the 1940s, when Christoff made his
début in Rome and was turning his gaze towards Covent
Garden and San Francisco, the fame of the great pre-war
opera singers had not yet faded. The glory of La Scala, Milan,
had not faded either. It had been destroyed by American
bombing on 3 August 1943, but the people were not
prepared to live without it. Italy quickly restored the theatre
even before the country had emerged from chaos, as if it saw
in La Scala a symbol of its artistic glory. On 11 May 1946, it
was reopened. This was a triumph not only of the old
sentiments but also of fresh hopes. Arturo Toscanini
returned from the United States to conduct the first concert.
The enthusiastic audience once again saw their old
favourites on the rebuilt stage: Mariano Stabile, Mafalda
Favero, Tancredi Pasero; and alongside them were the rising
stars: Renata Tebaldi, Mario Del Monaco and Nicola

Rossi-Lemeni were following the same path simultaneously with Christoff. In 1950 Callas made her début at La Scala.

During his rise to fame Christoff sang under the conductor Vittorio Gui, the first major conductor to offer him a friendly hand. They had met at Christoff's first concerts in Rome in 1945 on behalf of the Italo-Soviet society. Under Gui he sang for the first time at La Scala in the Brahms *Requiem* (during the concert season). During this period he also sang under Tullio Serafin, Gabriele Santini, Antonino Votto, and Franco Ghione, and in the years to come he crossed paths with many other musical giants. As early as 1949 he made recordings of arias from *Boris Godunov*. One year later, with Karajan, he recorded his unforgettable version of the aria of King Philip. In 1950 he made recordings with Issay Dobrowen of arias from *Prince Igor* and Rimsky-Korsakov's *Sadko*. In 1951 he took part in a performance of Verdi's *I vespri Siciliani* with the conductor Erich Kleiber (see Discography). In subsequent years his recording engagements were scarcely less numerous than his tours of the great opera houses.

Christoff was now mentioned in the same breath as Chaliapin. At the present time his fame is kept alive through his discs. Many of his admirers, who did not hear him at first hand, continue to thrill to his powerful and beautiful voice, his unusual dramatic range and the tragic images he conveyed. At the end of the 1940s Chaliapin's records, though not perfect from a technical point of view, were still in circulation. Documentary recordings made in 1928 of a performance of *Boris Godunov* at Covent Garden in which Chaliapin took part had also been preserved. It was on this same stage two decades later that Christoff won rapturous applause from the London public. When in the 1950s the critics asserted that Christoff was 'a genius of the lyric theatre', the 'best bass of our era' and even 'the tsar of basses', they were not flinching from comparisons with their memories of Chaliapin.

Christoff's immense reputation among critics, conductors and producers grew in spite of his reputation as a difficult, sometimes awkward person. After the incident with Peter Brook of Covent Garden in 1949, he fell out with one producer or another almost every season. His musical ideas, which in the eyes of many were crude or capricious, even led to the postponement of tours that would be the dream of any singer. In spite of that, with every fresh performance and concert, he increased his prestige and the number of his admirers and friends, even among the administrations he had angered.

Christoff's reputation rests not merely on the power of his voice but on its beautiful timbre, its rich colouring and emotional nuances. Innumerable critical reviews, written in so many languages have tried to define its special qualities. It is described as 'rich, lustrous with Slavonic overtones and finesse', 'beautiful in every nuance, in every condition, *piano* or *forte*, and in the lowest or highest notes', 'a magical voice, the timbre of which makes it recognizable amidst hundreds of others – noble, serious and inspiring'. In 1973 *The Times* critic stated that Christoff had 'the range of a baritone, although his timbre is that of a bass'. The same year, Vera Lempert wrote something similar in the Italian journal *Musica*: 'He is the greatest of those that possess that special timbre – sad and melancholy – which we call the "Slavonic bass".' And Howard Taubman in the *New York Times* in October 1956 wrote that 'his voice is a smooth and powerful bass with higher notes which have the resonance of a baritone'.

These opinions reveal to us, from different points of view,

the truth that Christoff has a genius for shading his voice, so that it is equally expressive whether he is praying or weeping or issuing commands; that his voice has exceptionally rich colouring, which is sometimes difficult to detect, as if it had been touched by the caress of a spring breeze. At other times it is packed with dramatic contrasts. But it is always accurately placed, with staggering assurance. It can cast a spell with its muted sighing; it can create lyrical sounds and communicate a sense of happiness with a unique *mezza voce*; it can achieve a steady and unshakeable bronze accuracy or an irresistible brilliance in magisterially controlled top notes.

These God-given vocal gifts are allied to a brilliant technique, which is also often mentioned in reviews. This technique includes his ability to observe the musical proprieties, to produce resonant *fortissimi*, to control the emotional values of each musical phrase and to discover the precise emphasis for climaxes. Reviews often refer to the phenomenon that when he sings on stage the audience is left breathless, enchanted by his interpretative skills and his personal magnetism, and that when his restrained, quiet and smooth voice is carried through the theatre scarcely anyone concerns himself with the technique that lies behind it. At this instant, the rich range of nuances and veiled tonal colouring is transformed into suffering, a groan, sighs or a prayer and the audience is overwhelmed by the downfall or ascent of the titanic character he is portraying. It is, in the highest degree, technique at the service of art.

From this point of view, also, Christoff may be compared with Chaliapin: in him, too, the singer and actor are inseparable. Many reviews of his opera performances and concerts refer to his massive stage presence, which is a product not only of his voice but of his dramatic gifts. In

1956, when the ovations Christoff received in Buenos Aires opera house 'exceeded anything that could be recalled in this theatre', the Argentine newspapers stressed that his portrayal of Boris Godunov was overwhelming not only from a vocal point of view but also in terms of his acting.

In Christoff's view the creation of a role on stage is a single-minded affair that cannot be achieved without what is known as 'engraving'. Among other things, this engraving requires self-analysis and an unusually varied amount of information – an expressive eye from one picture, a resonant phrase from some book, a characteristic facial expression from some striking individual. He was able to absorb and exploit this kind of information from his earliest days in opera, and in the course of time it became transformed into an enormous archive, everyday contact with which was essential. If one asks him for details about his roles, he might show you his own sketch for Dosifey, in which he sought to portray the expression of his own face; or he might pull out a score of *Khovanshchina* and thumb busily through its pages: 'Look! I made the Italian translation myself. That crown is for my part. Ecstasy. It was dramatic.... Slight pain or sighing.... It was a big crown! Lift your hands.... "Father! My heart is open to you." In Italian they put it well, and perhaps more beautifully: "Father, you know my soul ...".

He will show you reproductions of paintings from which he 'borrowed' something, or he will demonstrate a particular gesture from Philip II, or the way he had applied his make-up for the role. And he will do all this with the same enthusiasm he brings to preparing for a performance.

Naturally all this complex preparatory thought and work cannot be perceived on stage during a performance. But its results are accessible and clear to everyone present in the auditorium. Those who have viewed things more analytically

– the critics, performers and experts, including the luminaries on the conductor's podium – have often discovered that Christoff is able to delight even when he is not singing and that he can conquer with his presence alone. Assen Naidenov, the only Bulgarian who has faced Christoff from the conductor's podium, has vivid recollections of the experience: 'I had the good fortune to conduct him in four performances of Mussorgsky's *Boris Godunov* at the San Carlo Opera in Naples.... These performances revealed to me his true image and greatness as a man, singer and actor. It became clear that the great difference between him and other famous singers is his exceptional gift for acting. I even think that if he had not become a singer he could have been a dramatic actor. His technique when singing at performances and recitals is exemplary.... I know of no other singer capable of such aesthetic, artistic and spontaneous use of such powerfully effective tones and dynamic shading when he sings.... Richard Wagner said singing is refined speech. How appropriate that excellent concept is for the art of Boris Christoff! Is not his singing refined speech and his speech refined singing?

'In 1934 Feodor Chaliapin visited our country with his then chief conductor, Moisei Markovich Zlatin. To this day my recollections of him are alive and fresh. When it comes to the ability to handle the voice with a rich and comprehensive range of nuances and colouring, Boris Christoff is superior.'

Not the least of the factors that explain Christoff's spectacular success is his character, and his ability to arouse conflict and tension. At first glance such an assertion might seem puzzling since no one increases the number of his friends and admirers when he challenges them to a duel; but in fact this is just how things stand. Behind his conflicts lie differences of principle, and without such principles no significant art can exist. Very often he has quarrelled with precisely those people who are the most esteemed at that moment and who are responsible for taking very important decisions. But only his own peace of mind has suffered as a result – at no time has his prestige been affected. He has always let it be understood that he takes seriously the need to renew and enrich the artistic heritage of the past. In his own words, 'a respect for tradition does not mean conservatism'. His struggle to introduce the Russian language into performances of the classics of Russian music is proof of that.

He had no hesitation in turning down an invitation from the Paris Opéra to sing *Don Carlos* in French (the language Verdi envisaged for this opera) because he is convinced it sounds more correct and beautiful in Italian and because Verdi's characteristic phrasing is lost when it is not sung in Italian. He knows that modern technology provides opportunities to achieve rich scenic effects, but when he speaks of such opportunities he does not have in mind the gimmickry of the more frivolous producers.

As early as the 1950s, during his first visit to San Francisco, Christoff was in passionate conflict with the director of the company on whose orders the producer had shown him the set designs for *Boris Godunov* only three days before the dress rehearsal, even though they had long been prepared. Christoff was indignant and decided to take drastic action right after the first orchestral rehearsal for the final scenes. The basic cause was innocent enough, but the conductor was well aware of his insistence that he should be shown the designs at the very beginning and everyone was concerned at the danger of another dispute like that at Covent Garden.

At the moment when the orchestra had begun to play one of the most tender passages of the prayers of the dying Tsar, Christoff was not in accord with the views of the conductor and ceased singing. Since the conductor was of German extraction the singer approached him rather discreetly and cautiously with a request in German that these phrases should be sung in the very softest *pianissimi* since this had been laid down in Mussorgsky's score. In response, however, he received this angry reply:

'I am in command here. You will sing with the orchestra as I wish!'

Christoff retorted:

'It would be best if we were in command together. We are not in a barracks here and I cannot stand dictators.'

After curtly pronouncing these words he left the stage and shut himself in his dressing room. The effect was like the explosion of a bomb. Everyone was aghast. The director of the house and the conductor together rushed to the dressing room and began to shout and threaten the singer that if he made such scenes he would never be invited back to the United States. Then Christoff opened the door and standing at the threshold said: 'If all Americans are like you it would be just as you say. But fortunately it's not like that. You are violating the laws of art, about which there can be no argument. For more than 10 days you concealed from me this set design, which does not contain a single genuine Russian object. You have given responsibility for the designs to a person who has no understanding of the theatre or music and who is harming your professional and artistic reputation. This opera was created by Mussorgsky out of the story by Pushkin; its action takes place in a setting which can be found in Russia to the present day.

'Your fine conductor, instead of co-operating with the

singers, wishes to "command" them, which casts doubts on his theatrical and musical credentials. Positive results are achieved on stage only through intensive and calm work. In explanation of this I tell you that this pointless scene is bound to diminish the name of Mussorgsky and my own reputation for scrupulousness. If you do not change the sets for the scenes in which I take part, I shall regretfully leave San Francisco and return to Italy, where I have never yet come across such a distortion of musical theatre. Such things do not happen in Frascati!'

'But I am trying to get away from the out-dated style of the traditional Italian theatre,' said a rather calmer voice.

'That is where you went wrong!' interrupted Franca, who as always was on the side of her husband. 'Instead of trying to dream up such things, you should look again at how things are done in my country, without offending it and without angering my husband. Thank God, Boris, that we bought return tickets. If this scandal is not settled we shall take the first boat home.'

Sol Hurok, the impresario who had brought Christoff to San Francisco, did not disagree with the singer's views, perhaps because he realized that they were not capricious but the conditions of someone with high professional standards. He is not the only person to realize that. In the years that followed, there have been many such disagreements. Christoff quarrelled with artistic directors, conductors, designers and producers, not because he did not understand what they were trying to do, but because he did not wish to descend to their level. Despite the difficulties and outbursts of anger, for the most part they agreed with him. If all these incidents were collected and made into a book they would make amusing reading.

During rehearsals at Naples for a new production of *Attila* in 1973, the management of the opera house was changed. The newspapers wrote that everything would turn out well and looked forward to a good performance even though time was short. The conductor, Georges Prêtre, who had been on top of things, left and his successor was ill. The management appointed the chorus master to take complete control of rehearsals, but this had no effect. A dress rehearsal was arranged but on that day the chorus went on strike. Christoff, who was already in costume, had to wait. At the second dress rehearsal the members of the orchestra struck; and at the third, it was the firemen. Then all the soloists got together and decided not to appear in the first performance without the proper rehearsal time.

The management was informed of their decision. The next day, Christoff learnt in his hotel that he was expected at the opera house and that, despite everything, the performance was going ahead. One after another the strikers gave in until he was practically the only one holding out against artistic compromise. That evening he received a telegram dismissing him from the cast and informing him that he would be sued for causing moral and material harm to the opera house. Of course, that did not change his position and a case was brought against him which lasted eight months. He hired a lawyer and finally the court decided in his favour. On 30 October 1973, *Corriere della Sera* reported: 'San Carlo loses its fight with Christoff'.

He applied the same high standards when he was preparing to sing in Moscow. In fact, he was singing at the Bolshoi but only before members of the company engaged for *Boris Godunov* and some of their friends and relations. The orchestral rehearsal went brilliantly, straight through, and at the end all the musicians stood and applauded him, full of admiration for his masterly interpretation. The next day, however, the conductor had a heart attack and was replaced by a younger colleague. There was not enough time for proper rehearsals with him and many things needed to be worked out and corrected.

Only two days remained before the performance and Christoff was worried about going ahead with the engagement – he had dreamed too long of this moment to want to take risks. He could not sing before these demanding people in this famous theatre unless he felt confident in himself. Some such situation, or similar ones, occurred on other tours. They all arose as a consequence of his desire for perfection.

# 5

## Seeking Historical Truth

To have a correct understanding of the roles created by Boris Christoff, or rather to find the thread that connects them, we must remember that they embody the conflicts of the historical life of the people. The role played by the operas of Verdi in the period from the 1840s to the 1870s is one of the most eloquent illustrations of this. These operas brought to the attention of thousands of people images of heroic deeds, personal dramas and emotional conflicts. They tell of the suffering of the Jews in ancient times (*Nabucco*); the complex political intrigues of the Genoese republic in the 15th century (*Simone Boccanegra*); the struggle in Sicily in the 13th century against the French invaders (*I vespri Siciliani*); and the dramas of the Spanish court of the 17th century (*Don Carlos*).

When in *I Lombardi* the chorus of Crusaders sang as they set off to liberate Jerusalem, the audience in those days saw it as a call for the liberation of Italy herself. When in *Ernani* they sang of the glories of Iberia, the Italians transmuted it into the glories of Italy. The popular heroes of the past were now resurrected and imbued with the views of revolutionary romanticism so as to mobilize popular enthusiasm for the liberation and unification of Italy.

The première of *La battaglia di Legnano* took place only 10 days before the beginning of a true drama, played out in real life on the barricades of the popular uprising for the unification of Italy in 1849.

Nowadays there is no need to change the historically correct scene of their action, as Verdi was forced to do – to substitute the Netherlands for Italy, and Portugal for Sicily. The successors of the forces which in 1857 delayed the Naples première of *Un Ballo in maschera* are, however, still alive. Or rather, the vices, intrigues and envy that can create desperate situations and conflicts still remain. When Christoff portrays the bass roles in these works so responsibly and authentically, he returns to them their strength as characters.

In the 1950s his name was particularly associated with the roles of Oroveso in Bellini's *Norma*, Moses in Rossini's *Mosè* and Colline in Puccini's *La Bohème*. During the same period his repertoire was also closely linked with the works of Verdi: with growing success he performed the roles of Ramfis in *Aïda*, Silva in *Ernani*, King Philip in *Don Carlos*, Padre Guardiano in *La Forza del destino*, Fiesco in *Simone Boccanegra*, Giovanni da Procida in *I vespri Siciliani* and Banquo in *Macbeth*. Something more than personal ambition and the demands of the moment must lie behind such a speedy and broad commitment. Clearly in this case it was a question of a naturally creative disposition. Although his Slavonic character sometimes clashed powerfully with the

'Western' romanticism of these masterpieces, his musicianly gifts were never in doubt, and he interpreted the notes with an authenticity and inspiration that few others have been able to equal.

On various occasions Christoff has told friends, musicologists and journalists that he divides operas that deal with characters and events from the past into two groups: those based on true historical facts and those with literary or imaginary heroes. He cannot restrict himself to the libretto to arrive at a true interpretation of these operas. He needs a knowledge of the epoch and of the characters that he has to portray. That means he also needs an accurate feel for the nature of the personal relationships in specific circumstances. In other words, he does not begin by learning the score, but by studying the period and the complexity of the characters, particularly when information about them is sparse. Old editions of the work can be a great help – they can bring us closer to the spirit of the past. When that can be achieved all one's efforts must be concentrated on the intentions of the composer. A correctly integrated role must be portrayed on stage just as the composer conceived it.

It is generally recognized that King Philip II in Verdi's *Don Carlos* is one of Christoff's greatest roles. He has performed it on the stages of the greatest opera houses in the world – Rome, Milan, London, Paris, Vienna, Budapest, Madrid, Buenos Aires and Copenhagen – from 1950 to the present day. He has given more than 420 performances of Philip II alone. Christoff has the ability accurately and comprehensively to portray the traditional concept of the complex and gloomy despot consumed by contradictions, adding fresh nuances and insights to his interpretation over the years.

In Vienna in 1963 they played down the question of the sword in the Inquisition scene, showing the public clash between Philip II and Don Carlos. Christoff was horrified that the producer had envisaged that the sword should appear briefly in the scene above the heads of the principals and pointed out that Verdi had not intended any such thing. At first glance this might seem to be a storm in a teacup, but for Christoff it was a question of fidelity to Verdi. In the end Christoff's exacting standards prevailed, even though he did not oppose the overall concept of the producer – a former ballerina – and declared that 'she is obliged to make theatre with whatever means she can'. Karajan, the conductor, declared a truce and when, on the first night, the audience greeted the production with rapturous applause, he withdrew the entire cast behind the curtain and sent out Christoff to take his call alone. Afterwards he went up to him and kissed him.

King Philip is morose and withdrawn. His self-confidence as a despot is shattered by suspicion and a sense of mortality (literally, the mortal space in which he lives) without the love of his young wife, without the friendship of Don Rodrigo and alienated from his own son, Don Carlos. He is the personification not only of profound psychological conflicts but also of a personal drama of complex emotions. All of this has been revealed in thousands of ways by more or less talented singers. Christoff, while accepting this conception of the role, does not treat it as holy writ, rather as an idea that must be transformed into an image, just as the notation is transformed into music. The image is always that of Christoff himself on stage, since his wish to be to some extent co-author, producer and editor is quite legitimate. Hence there are changing nuances in all his portrayals of the role, since he tries not to repeat other singers' interpretations or his own. He does this instinctively, so that reviewers have always discovered fresh ideas in his interpretation.

I first heard Christoff sing King Philip's Monologue II on a 78 rpm record at the beginning of the 1950s. I was studying at Moscow University, and the record was played on a cheap gramophone in my little room in the skyscraper on the Lenin Hills. For me and some of my acquaintances it became so precious that when it grew worn from use we were oblivious to its defects. When I first came to know Christoff, in Paris in December 1966, he was singing the role of King Philip II. I recall that in Act 3, Christoff's voice emerged from the orchestra, low-pitched, gliding over the dark expanses. His hollow notes filled out, rose energetically, dissolved into a whispered, suppressed *mezza voce*. Later they became a powerful and terrible symbol of torment, of fear and despair. The auditorium remained silent as if it had withdrawn in terror from this emotional torrent. Sorrow in the world of kings: the voice of personal tragedy sighed again and was transformed into a cry of farewell, became lower, began again for a moment and then reached a terrifying pause. It was as if everything had sunk into the depths – the voice, the orchestra, the stage and everyone in the auditorium.

In *Don Carlos* Verdi reached a new level in combining the orchestra and voice. At this moment in Paris, however, I thought that this combination had been created by Christoff himself because he changed and inflected his voice like an instrumental accompaniment: he emerged from the orchestra as if he were opening it up to himself, infecting it with his grief, imposing his rhythm upon it, driving it to moan, to play louder and more energetically, to fade away in despair in the depths into which he himself had subsided.

At that instant my mind went back not to the voice on that worn old record but to the galleries of the Prado gallery in Madrid in which are the portraits of the despots, princes, infantas and cardinals that are the subject of the opera.

Under the brush of Velasquez or of El Greco they are transformed into images displaying not their power but their human characteristics.

In his role Christoff seemed not to act but to suffer, and everyone was convinced by him. When the curtain came down the audience did not break out immediately into wild applause, but expressed its appreciation with the same noble simplicity and clarity.

After the performance I went to congratulate Christoff in his dressing-room; I was his only Bulgarian acquaintance. In front of the dressing-room an enormous queue of people was waiting; all had been mesmerized as if under the influence of forces over which they had no control.

Christoff greeted his guests sitting down, free from any airs, as if there had not been a stage, or ovations after the final curtain. Still in his make-up and costume, he was collected and attentive, but on his face was a natural lively expression that can be neither acquired nor simulated. Most of the people were waiting for autographs, but he was in no hurry to take the programmes and photographs offered. I was able to observe how anxious people were to share a few words with him, or perhaps to hear from him why they had waited for something which would belong to them for ever.

Lengthy reviews appeared in *Le Figaro*, *Combat*, *Paris Presse* and *Le Nouvel Observateur*. Many of the impressions and conclusions they contained were fully in accord with what one might have heard in the dressing-room at the Opéra. *Le Figaro*'s critic wrote that 'from his head to his toes, Boris Christoff is Philip II and he transfixes and overwhelms us with his cold and sombre gaze. When we see him upon the stage with his melancholy gestures and commanding profile, we accept him not as Boris Christoff the singer but always as Philip II of Spain.' His performance evoked a similar response in the other critics. Bernard Gavoty, for example, wrote that if the stature, form or physical image of glory exists, then 'Boris Christoff truly possesses that stature and that physique'.

The visitors to his dressing-room had had the opportunity to witness another performance: he had continued to enrich them with what they had already discovered on stage. Now his hands no longer trembled from pain and fury, but his enormous eyes continued to overwhelm one with the same power and intensity. His bronzed face with its finely sculptured features was welcoming and, along with his words, suggested a brilliant spiritual richness. Here, in a flash, many of us discovered that Christoff went on stage not merely with his vocal technique but with a wisdom and charm which he carried within himself, and that the brilliance and substance of his Philip II was determined solely by his personal spiritual and physical presence, not by properties, costumes or lighting effects.

On 14 December 1966, Gavoty came upon Christoff in rehearsal for *Don Carlos* at the Palais Garnier, and on the following day described for his readers how he had been present at an unusual event. 'In the fourth scene', he wrote, 'there comes a moment when Don Carlos points his sword at the king, because of his refusal to allow him to rule Flanders. With rising anger the king three times gives orders that he should be disarmed. The traditional *mise-en-scène* lays down that at this precise moment a page with timely foresight should bring Philip a sword neatly placed upon a red cushion. "That's stupid!" Christoff exploded. "Dear friends, if you need a sword, let me tell you a king never carries a sword. A sword! Here it is!" With a tigerish leap the singer threw himself upon a nearby soldier, placed his hand on his shoulder and withdrew the sword that was hanging from his belt. In surprise the page allowed the sword to fall from the embroidered cushion. Clearly the scene had acquired a new angle.'

This curious story furnishes yet another example of Christoff's determination to preserve the 'holy flame' in everything connected with him on stage: his striving to be natural and, in the name of that truthfulness to nature, to reject if need be even the most time-honoured theatrical conventions. 'I am not only a singer,' he would insist, and the journalists fully understood him. Indeed, one of them titled his article in *Paris Presse* 'This Boris Christoff, who is not only a singer'. Under this headline he wrote enthusiastically that Christoff's voice is not only beautiful but magnificent and that his successes on the operatic stage are based upon human principles. How this is to be understood more clearly is explained by these thoughts of the singer himself: 'Nowadays everyone sings with a microphone at his lips. But an operatic artist interprets.... His own task is determined by the level of the image he is portraying on stage.'

Some years later, in Rome, I had many opportunities to hear Christoff's views about *Don Carlos*. They were given haphazardly, on various occasions, but whenever he spoke of his favourite role of Philip II, he said something of substance. He spoke of the need for a broad education, internal conviction and a love of the truth.

'With Wagner the voice is lost in the orchestra.... It is true that there are moments when it slips out and rises above it.... arias in which the genius of Wagner can be strongly felt occur. But afterwards the vocal line is again drowned by the orchestra. Verdi is down to earth. He creates dramatic situations and they have to be interpreted clearly. Everything is important with him. On stage everything can be transformed into art only with the aid of training, education and innate talent....'

The sum total of roles which Christoff has sung since the late 1940s makes a formidable list. Apart from the heritage of Verdi he has discovered greatly loved roles and subjects in the works of dozens of other composers. Thus his musical biography includes such notable interpretations as Henry the Fowler in *Lohengrin*; Oroveso in Bellini's *Norma*; the gold merchant in Hindemith's *Cardillac*; Count Robinson in Cimarosa's *Il matrimonio segreto*; Hagen in *Götterdämmerung*; Giorgio in Bellini's *I Puritani*; Rocco and Pizarro in *Fidelio*; Seneca in Monteverdi's *L'Incoronazione di Poppea*; Mephistophélès in Gounod's *Faust*; Agamemnon in Gluck's *Iphigénie en Aulide*; Creon in Gluck's *Orfeo ed Euridice*; the title role in Rossini's *Mosè*; Julius Caesar in Handel's opera of the same name; Gurnemanz in *Parsifal*; the title role in Boito's *Mefistofele*; Don Basilio in *Il barbiere di Siviglia*; Caspar in Weber's *Der Freischütz*; King Saul in Nielsen's *Saul and David*; Henry VIII in Donizetti's *Anna Bolena*; and many others.

Several of these operas did not remain long in the repertoire of the houses in which they were performed. They were rarities whose renaissance was greatly helped by Christoff's participation, a fact abundantly proved by the reviews of his performances.

In 1959 when Christoff sang the role of Moses for the first time at the Rome Opera House a critic wrote: 'It is a bold undertaking to present an opera like *Mosè* as it should be done.... A performer with an astonishing musical and psychological perception was the bass Boris Christoff, who not for the first time won our admiration. He was able to breathe life into the vast, sculptured figure of Moses. He removed it from its pedestal and with the aid of the music he made of it a living being. With his warm and winning voice and his idiosyncratic way of shaping the words he was able to bestow upon Rossini's Moses his perfect image both from a dramatic and a musical point of view.' The *Vitox Post* wrote of Christoff's portrayal of Moses with the same enthusiasm: 'As Moses, Christoff, a man of medium height, was an imposing figure, from the point of view both of his voice and his personality. Whether he was the enraged Moses who had brought about the fall of darkness or the unshakeable man of faith foretelling that the Lord would remove the chains of slavery from his people, he was dynamically communicative. Without costume or elaborate set Christoff, with enormous strength and power, evoked the personality of the great leader of the Jews who liberated his people from slavery. Through his voice and artistic skill he portrayed both the leader and the people.'

Many years later the interest in this magnificent portrayal had still not subsided. In a review in *The Times* of 13 April 1971, the musicologist Jeremy Noble wrote that 'on the stage of the Rome Opera House Boris Christoff has created for the second time a unique Moses.... He did not descend to the generally accepted interpretation – the cliché of the "spiritual leader". The character of his Moses was quite different from that of his Dosifey. He portrayed, with his acting and singing, an active, even impulsive old man without a trace of Russian mysticism in the part.'

At the beginning of June 1984, we were discussing in Rome the gallery of giants he had portrayed up to that moment and their complex artistic character. When the subject of Moses came up a large black-and-white photograph of the well-known statue by Michelangelo appeared on the table before us. A few hours earlier this photograph had been unearthed in a bookshop near San Pietro and purchased both in the hope that it might at some time be needed for some publication but also simply for its inherent qualities. It lay near a pile of similar reproductions, unnoticed at that time; but when the conversation turned to Moses it was all at once brought forward as something of significance. Christoff was pleasantly surprised: 'When I played Moses for the first time at the Maggio Musicale Fiorentino I worked with Tullio Serafin. At that time I studied the Moses of Michelangelo very carefully, and I took fright. How could I recreate such a giant? Some singers even imitated the outward appearance of this image, but is that really the most important factor? My first reaction was to take two steps backward. At close quarters his grandeur altered.... Later I decided to follow my own conception.'

As he spoke, he drew the photograph close to himself and then moved it away, then he stood upright and leant over it as if he was once again feeling the responsibility of portraying the Biblical leader. I had looked at Michelangelo's masterly statue in San Pietro in Vincoli dozens of times but I had never imagined that a singer would stand before it for so long and with such concentration. Now he saw in it his creative youth, his happy hours with Serafin and his concept of greatness and spiritual power.

When it came to Mephistophélès in Gounod's *Faust*, Christoff spent a lot of time on creating his own interpretation. 'I racked my brains over this role,' he admitted. 'Goethe had to be borne in mind. But how to begin? Marguerite and her feelings were understandable. But what was the essence of this cavalier: purely diabolic or also with human characteristics? The desire of an old man – Faust – to become young again stirred me.... But other things also attracted me. I liked very much the Serenade in which satanic power could be felt. It was good that the wrestling was not in vain. My portrayal had clearly been liked. I made two recordings of *Faust* for EMI.'

One critic commented: 'We looked forward with a certain curiosity to the appearance of this singer with the exceptional vocal and artistic gifts. We did not doubt his intelligence, but we wanted to discover to what extent and with what results this intelligence would allow him to make the transition from the many varied roles in which we had heard him to the role of Mephistophélès. The transition was excellent and the achievement superb. With his interpretation of this role Christoff confirmed his great acting and vocal skills. He demonstrated how to enrich natural gifts with intelligence and unwavering tenacity in learning. He is a rare example, and many young and not so young singers who are accustomed to making use of superficial effects should learn from him. With his astoundingly lively, graceful and overpowering acting, with the facial expression of a great actor, he achieved an interpretation of Mephistophélès which we can describe without reservation as the best we have heard to date.... It was as if he had really concluded a pact with the devil in order to portray it so magnificently. Every fresh interpretation of this true master of the stage amazes and arouses unrestrained admiration.'

*Il Tempo* wrote of his Agamemnon in Gluck's *Iphigénie en Aulide*, which Christoff first sang in 1954: 'As always Boris Christoff showed himself to be a colossus. It is not easy on the operatic stage to achieve the precise equilibrium between the classical spirit and intensity of accent which Boris Christoff was able to achieve in the role of Agamemnon. It seemed that the tragedy that lies in the music of *Iphigénie* emanated mainly from his person. It did this so brilliantly that one could no longer distinguish the singer from the actor or the music from the drama. It seemed this was exactly what Gluck intended. Scenes like the one I would call the scene of remorse, with its long recitative in which every syllable and shudder can be heard, are destined to remain in the memory for years.'

In 1956 critics wrote of his Don Basilio in *Barbiere*: 'With his giant stature as a singer Boris Christoff left all the rest behind. His Don Basilio was elevated to almost Biblical proportions. The grotesque in the interpretation was strongly stressed but without depriving the character of his human qualities. He revealed the content of the Slander aria with noteworthy gracefulness and secure accents and this brought him deserved success.'

In 1955, Guido Pannain wrote of Christoff's participation in Handel's *Giulio Cesare*: 'With astounding harmony Boris Christoff portrayed the role of a Julius Caesar ... who has purely human characteristics ... a Caesar brought to life through the music as dramatic incarnation demands. With his delicate and unique *mezza voce*, his fine tone, and dramatic gifts, Christoff proved himself an exceptional performer.'

A critic wrote of Christoff's performance in *Parsifal* at La Scala in 1960: 'So far as Boris Christoff, who played the difficult role of Gurnemanz, is concerned, one can only say that he succeeded in conveying the authority of his role. This will remain in our memories as one of the happiest achievements of last night's performance.'

Books play an important part in the life of Christoff. They are the key to many questions about the development of his characters. All the virtues that entrance us on stage – his capacity to astonish us with his 'thunderous *fortissimi*' or with a restrained *mezza voce*, or his ability to shake us with the suffering of the powerful who have become the victims of their own conscience – derive from his knowledge of the past. When I saw his library for the first time I was slightly taken aback. It contains more than five thousand volumes which are always open, even if only in his subconscious. He can skim through their pages for days on end, forgetting all other cares, consult them with the aid of a little step-ladder, and read aloud pages that he knows as well as he knows his own life.

' "The Rhinoceros" 1750. Look at these engravings! Fabrizio Carozo da Sermonte. *The Dancer*, Venice 1580. It really is a pleasure for a man to own such things. These madrigals by Pietro Pache? Look ... Venice, 1616. Eh, you must know about this! These really are the basics ... Francesco Rognoni – *The Manual for Good Singing*, 1620. I think that this is the only copy in Italy!'

With this book in his hand, Christoff can sit on the sofa in his library and ignore the passage of time. At such moments I would occasionally ask him how he had managed to collect all these valuable volumes, but I realized that this was not very significant since he did not hurry to reply. In the event it was his attitude towards them that mattered and about that he did have something to say.

'Imagine ... Florence 1545. *Vicerio in musica di alcune openioni*.... What is that about? When a man buys something, he must know what he needs. Listen. Rognoni, *Manual* of 1620.... It pleases me to know that people used to sing in a cultivated manner even 300 years ago and that they knew what only few people know today.'

He said this as if he were speaking to himself, rather like a traveller setting off into the distant unknown, and I realized that on such a journey one really does not need company. It was a journey into human thought and the European culture of several centuries. His library must be one of the richest private collections of its kind in the world. When he thumbs through his books he is in fact travelling through the suffering and insights of generations – through engravings for

Dante's *Inferno*, through the illustrations for *A Journey to Russia*, 1718, through the lessons of Ottavio Valera or through *The Synagogue of the Stupid*, published in Venice in 1589.

Of course, in shaping his roles he has to overcome many prejudices and old-fashioned traditions, which leads to conflict and unnecessary expenditure of time and effort. I remember how long it took him to arrive at his concept of Henry VIII in Donizetti's *Anna Bolena*, and not because it was one of his more difficult roles. On this occasion the difficulties were of a different nature, but in the end it was once again a question of creative analysis. As usual, he began to study his part seriously and responsibly, giving himself sufficient time to do so.

As a result of this analysis, he came to the conclusion that the opera was far too long and that its action developed in a rather monotonous manner; unless the producer actively intervened the production would turn out to be lifeless and banal. So he discussed the matter with the producer, Filippo Crivelli, and the conductor, Gabriele Ferro. They, however, were not prepared to listen to his ideas for shortening the work. That deeply disturbed him. I heard from him several times about these disputes and I became more and more convinced that it was not a question of prestige but rather one of creative standards that disturbed him. Some time, at the end of March 1977, only a few days before the opening night, we had a conversation at the Bulgarian embassy in Rome. He could not control himself: his anger was such that it could overcome everyone and everything.

'I am very upset. We have been preparing for the first night for more than 20 days, and recently it became clear that if the opera is not shortened we shall all suffer – performers and public alike. At first the producer promised to think of something. Now he is not prepared to do anything. It's unbelievable. I told him – that is not the way art should be interpreted.

'When the work was first given, the audience was free to roam about the theatre. Behind the boxes were salons in which the aristocracy could take refreshments without worrying whether they had missed anything. These works by Donizetti are not so often performed as, say, Rossini's *Mosè*: they are rarely given and then almost always in shortened versions. The producer speaks of tradition, but it does not exist. I have seen one of my old teachers and he said the same thing. Therefore I think that the opera must be up-dated or better still shortened. The moment when the sentence is pronounced is the climax. The sentence is death! After that there is no point in singing a long sextet – a long and boring sextet which kills the character of Henry VIII as an actor.'

I knew that Christoff's words were not wholly accurate. The opera *Anna Bolena* had not been forgotten in recent times and attempts to perform it had been made. It had been performed during the 1956–7 season at La Scala by Luchino Visconti with Maria Callas, Giulietta Simionato and Nicola Rossi-Lemeni. A new production at the Rome Opera House had made use of the designs and costumes of Nicola Benois among others and had taken note of the concept of Luchino Visconti, who had worked on the production with him 20 years earlier. In addition a recording had been made in 1969 by the Greek soprano Elena Suliotis with the chorus and orchestra of the Vienna State Opera, and in 1972 a second recording had been made with Beverly Sills and Shirley Verrett, Paul Plishka and the London Symphony Orchestra.

The critics had, however, expressed regret that Anna Bolena had not been sung by such an interpreter of the role

As Boris Godunov in various revivals at Covent Garden, where
Christoff had a triumphant career spanning over thirty years.
(Reg Wilson) (Donald Southern) (Zöe Dominic)

In the title role of Handel's *Guilio Cesare*, Rome, 1955. (*Opera*)

In the title role of Boito's *Mefistofele*, Chicago, 1961. (*Nancy Sorensen, Lyric Opera of Chicago*)

As Agamemnon in Gluck's *Iphigénie en Aulide*, La Scala, 1959. (*Opera*)

As Kochubey in Tchaikovsky's *Mazeppa*, Maggio Musicale, Florence, 1954. (*Opera*)

as Callas. In other words, they were implying that to bring the opera up to date something still remained to be done. So there was no reason to doubt that Christoff was right. He had in mind not just the modernization of the opera but also the need to portray the characters in a more lively fashion and to do away with repeats that do not carry forward the plot. He wanted the principals to develop in more lively, dynamic and convincing a manner so as to achieve a greater dramatic intensity and a cleaner style for the entire production. Unfortunately at that time his wish could not be realized. The management of the theatre underestimated the difficulties of achieving harmony among the cast, and although all the singers, including Christoff, rehearsed daily, the soprano singing Anna Bolena, Leyla Gencer, waited until the day before the first night before appearing at a rehearsal. For Christoff that was the bottom line.

'This is utterly irresponsible! I know that the producer is seriously worried. Not long ago he said in an interview that another opera he had produced had failed. I told him directly that opera must be treated as a serious art form. How could they have this attitude?'

He became red in the face and breathless when he spoke of this, as if he were deciding issues vitally affecting his life. The Rome Opera House had an obvious failure with its new production. When the final curtain fell the audience was indifferent. Christoff was not among the singers who took their bows in a rather embarrassed manner. He declared, 'Forgotten operas cannot be revived unless their basic faults are cleaned up.' This was the verdict of the Rome press on the next day. Christoff refused to take part in any further performances, although the director of the opera house offered to make cuts. It was too late to save the production.

# 6

---

## *Russian Opera*

The Russian repertoire occupies a central position in Christoff's artistic biography: the vivid characters of Russian operas and the heartfelt songs he has sung and recorded for more than 40 years. Merely to enumerate all these interpretations is enough to give one pause: it is so unlikely that one man alone could be capable of performing them. To collect and learn the hundreds of songs by Glinka, Rachmaninov, Mussorgsky, Balakirev, Rimsky-Korsakov, Cui or Tchaikovsky as well as to make a similarly thorough study of Russian classical operas, including those that are little known in the West, and to popularize them to such an extent, is not just a matter of talent and internal organization but also of a higher ideal.

Over a surprisingly short period, from the end of the 1940s to the beginning of the 1960s, when Europe was still clearing the burnt-out skeletons of once beautiful buildings from its streets and covering the scars caused by bombs and shells with broad expanses of grass, Christoff was able to fortify and embellish the spiritual life of many people with the sincerity of his performances of Russian music. His successful appearances on the stages of the most famous opera houses and his recordings of Russian music, which quickly achieved large sales, proved to be major events in the musical life of the era.

What he did was new, bold and inimitable. Admiration for his stylish and heartfelt interpretations and the potential of his voice mingled with admiration for the new tendencies and the nationalistic colouring in Glinka's music or the power and vividness of the five composers of the 'Mighty Handful'. He performed their masterpieces so conscientiously that they might have been written specially for him, and he returned to them afresh with ardent feelings and unlimited belief in the necessity of what he had begun.

One of the first roles in Christoff's Russian gallery was Ivan Susanin, from Glinka's opera of the same name (also known as *A Life for the Tsar*). He sang in this opera at La Scala in 1959, and his success resounded through Italian artistic circles for a long time. The critics wrote that at last, after a 123-year-long silence, the masterpiece of Glinka, the founder of Russian national musical drama, had been performed at La Scala. They could only regret this delay, because this masterpiece had introduced them to something without precedent in the annals of opera in European music: a protagonist with a vivid character and epic resonance.

The credit does not belong to Christoff alone, of course. The rave reviews in the press referred in the first place to Glinka and his opera. Furthermore, when the critics said that the dazzling performances at La Scala were unique and durable, they were also referring to the harmonious production of Tatiana Pavlova, the passionate inspiration and at the same time disciplined command of musical values of the conductor, Efrem Kurtz, the fascinating set and costumes by Benois, the magnificent choreography by Massine, and last but not least the achievements of the chorus and all the soloists: Renata Scotto, Fiorenza Cossotto and Gianni Raimondi.

Christoff's consistency in his interpretation of Ivan Susanin was much praised in all the musical journals of that time. Any researcher, going back to the musical life of those years, can find ample evidence of this. In building up this role Christoff relied largely upon his intuition. Glinka would have been the first to give him the right to do so. After all, it was he who said, 'Music is created by the people and we, the composers, only arrange it.' Christoff, too, made every attempt to touch upon the musical treasures of the people and to find his own way through the mystery of its voices and its colourful melodies. He needed first to inhale the authentic air of the period, to capture with the help of old publications the true sense of the pain, the laughter and the ecstasy of the people.

In his library there are numerous musical sketches of hunting music from Russia. One volume, published by Johann Christian Henricks in St Petersburg in the 18th century, contains many such themes together with the scores for all the separate instruments. In another publication entitled *Kaliki Perekhozhiye* by P. Bessonov he discovered 'Glinka's spirit', and in the collection of *Russian Folk Songs* published in 1812 he found 'one half of *Khovanshchina* with the songs of Marfa and the Streltsi'. He was not only pleased by these discoveries but was also aware that, in order to draw so boldly from the depths of the folk spirit and folk music, one requires a great talent. In other words, one requires a sense of innovation, adherence to the truth and the courage to turn one's back on all the fossilized forms of 'high' society with all its superficiality and gloss. For Christoff this courage became a criterion and he did not hesitate to extend the sense of continuity to himself in search of his interpretation without harming the style and spirit of Glinka.

'The peasant wedding of Antonida,' Teodoro Celli wrote in *Oggi*, 'Susanin bidding farewell to his children, and above all the meditation of the heroic peasant during the night in the forest ("Come out, O dawn, so that my eyes can see you for the last time") – these are all pages belonging to the great art of all time. They aroused the enthusiasm of the Scala audience. We have to give credit to Renata Scotto for her vocally brilliant Antonida and above all to Boris Christoff with his deep melancholy voice, with its mystic nuances, who gave us a brilliant interpretation of the heroic and at the same time deeply emotional soul of the peasant who gave his life for the Tsar.'

The review by Guido Pannain was even more enthusiastic: 'The figure of Ivan Susanin is shaped by accents that at first seem to have a traditional sound, a fake, rhetorical Rossini. Suddenly, however, there comes a radical change. In the scene in which Susanin bids farewell to the forest in anticipation of his forthcoming sacrifice, Christoff's voice becomes inspired. The suffering is released by memories relived. In this scene the strength of the performer becomes as one with the overall artistic conception and Boris Christoff showed himself to be the perfect interpreter. His singing was the reflection of inner contemplation. This is no longer the voice of a singing bass, but the song itself transformed into poetry.'

Christoff's portrayal of Boris Godunov is so captivating and vivid that many people tend to perceive it as a symbol encompassing two personalities. One of the most authoritative musicologists, Guido Pannain, asserted that 'Whenever the name of Modeste Mussorgsky is mentioned we automatically imagine Boris Christoff standing next to him.' It is certainly true that Christoff has always felt a desire to be close to Mussorgsky. He cherished the desire to see the composer as a part of himself, a part of his spirit, to have him in his everyday life, in his thoughts and in his plans.

At the time of the first ovations for his participation in *Boris Godunov* he had completed his colossal preparations for his recording of all of Mussorgsky's songs. It is difficult to say whether he became so closely associated with the role of Tsar Boris because of his fascination with Mussorgsky or vice versa.

Christoff was fully aware of the smear campaign that plagued Mussorgsky, who was accused of being 'a drunk and a rascal', 'obsessed with chaotic effects and dissonance', and of leaving 'a barbaric heritage, to the shame of the whole of Russia'. These accusations in the pages of *Birzhoviye Vedomosti* and *Russky Mir* became a source of shame to generations of cultured Russians. Christoff ignored them. If he ever felt the need to rebut such calumnies, he would know where to seek reliable moral support. His allies are Rimsky-Korsakov and the other members of the 'Mighty Handful' – Balakirev, Borodin and Cui, not to mention Liszt, who said he had been 'overwhelmed by Mussorgsky's work'.

What Christoff appreciates most is the fact that Mussorgsky has such a truthful sense of the spirit of the Russian people. He appreciates the fact that Mussorgsky enlarges on Pushkin by including the scene of the Kromy rebellion; that he had set out on a bold search for new forms that would enable him to reveal the true feelings of the ordinary Russian people; that he had dared to break away from the structure of the classical aria in favour of virtuoso handling of the free monologue; and that his shady life in the taverns and slums helped him 'to become the most truly Russian composer among his contemporaries'. All of this captivates and inspires Christoff like an ideal of unattainable beauty, or like a religion one should follow with absolute dedication. A reproduction of the famous portrait of Mussorgsky by Repin hangs in a prominent position in his study.

The scores of *Boris Godunov* and the 'Sunless' cycle are always open upon his piano as though awaiting their composer, who might turn up at any moment and sit down in front of them as if he were in his own house. Some antique dealers that Christoff once knew presented him with the original drawing of Repin for the cover of the first edition of Mussorgsky's 'Nursery' cycle: another sacred relic, exuding the aura of the times when the 'Mighty Handful' were breaking new ground in Russian music.

Christoff likes to share the ecstatic inspiration he obtains from the composer when people are prepared to sit and listen to him. He expressed some of his thoughts about Mussorgsky in an article published in the *Musical Encyclopedia Ricordi*, 1963: 'Mussorgsky is completely isolated from the other composers of the past, as well as from his contemporaries. His aesthetic is completely at odds with that of the "pure music": it remains alien to the monumental Western music, it avoids the traditional polyphonies, forms, rhythms, structures, etc.; its only sources are the language and the soul of his nation, regardless of social classes ... the only thing that truly matters to him is to re-create man by means of music.'

To appreciate and understand the nature of the characters

created by Mussorgsky would appear to be easy only to those who are unaware of their complexity. In many English-language reviews Boris Godunov has been called the Russian Macbeth or the Russian Richard III. To describe him as a psychological and behavioural type is one thing, but the effort to embody him, 'taking responsibility' for his sins and rages, tenderness and agonies, is a totally different matter. For Christoff it is not enough to extract his personality only from the scores, from the deliberations of the critics, and from previous interpretations by others, no matter how perceptive these may be. His goal is not simply to put on the garments of the various characters, but to truly re-create them in full blood, to make them alive and believable.

There is only one road one can take to achieve this, and it leads to the epoch inhabited by Mussorgsky's characters. It passes by the golden domes of the churches, awakening the sleepy forests with their endless chimes; it passes through the fanaticism of the Old Believers and goes down into the wooden huts in which the suffering conscience of the time is hiding. This road is not mapped out in the engravings Christoff buys nor in the old publications that he consults, and there is no guarantee that one would not miss what one is seeking. But, for Christoff, there is no choice. The necessary visual material can be gathered only from such sources as the expression in the eyes of the hunchback in Repin's painting, *The Holy Way*, the gestures of the idiot sitting half naked in the snow in *The Boyarka Morozova* by Surikov, the intonations in the songs collected by Bessonov in *Kaliki Perekhozhiye*, the intriguing engravings in a book published in 1718 in Amsterdam under the title of *The Travels of Corneille le Brun around Moscow, Persia and the East Indies*.

Creating the interpretation requires not only experience, intuition and courage, but in addition a good deal of luck, self-control and self-knowledge. It is no wonder that by the time it first appears on stage, and even afterwards, the role has not always been drawn with distinct lines. At the beginning Christoff was only gravitating around Boris Godunov: he was first cast as Pimen. Next came the offer to sing the role of Boris Godunov and to record all the three main bass parts (Boris, Varlaam and Pimen) in the opera. But was that a great opportunity, or perhaps a deception? One of his close friends from that time, the conductor Issay Dobrowen, sat at the piano and suggested that they should begin recording. But what about the risk? Dobrowen urged that he should sing Pimen and Varlaam as well as Boris. Christoff retired to his room in a Paris hotel and drew the curtains: he was wrapped in thought about faraway things. Would his boldness be appreciated? Three days later the curtains in his room were drawn back again, and the answer was in the affirmative. However, the anxieties about difficulties remained. The hard work was only just beginning for him. Perhaps, also, the real learning was only just beginning. By that time Labinsky and Sanin had just joined him.

Later, after his second recording of the opera, at the time when Paris was eagerly awaiting Christoff's appearance in the role of the tragic Tsar on the stage of the Opéra in September 1962, the musicologist Marcel Clavery wrote in *Combat* about Christoff's sense of responsibility and the profundity of his ideas: 'Boris Christoff once again explained the result so far achieved only by him – singing the three bass parts. These are three distinctly different parts, which he has differentiated in character (as in the previous recording) by novel use of musical colouring and recitation. The one element they have in common is the beauty of the timbre.

' "But why do you have to treble your difficulties?"'

' "To bring these three characters as close as possible to my own ideas of Mussorgsky, I have plunged into the depths of his music. I have sung all his works. Absolutely all of them, at least all of those written for my voice range. Apart from that I have carefully studied the ones outside my voice range, seeking in them the most secret details. I have performed 63 songs written by him and have directed my research further afield than the ordinary scores. I think that that gave me the opportunity to penetrate his most profound concepts. It became possible to interpret the three parts thanks to the possibilities offered by recording."

' "Have you changed your attitude since the previous recording?"

' "No, not at all. Several years ago my understanding of Boris, Pimen and Varlaam was exactly the same as it is today. Let's take Boris, for example: I do not take Pushkin, who emphasizes the murderer in him. I go with Mussorgsky, who, developing the theme in his opera, puts forward the humane side. Boris is no more than a man, sated with power and blood. He loves children. He is a believer. He is a thinker. And the burden on his conscience of the crimes he has committed kills him. This is the prevailing theme of Mussorgsky's opera. It is the spectacle of a gigantic, devastating tragedy of conscience, which can only kill the suffering soul of a repentant man. Boris dies because he has become a martyr. I have always seen it that way."

' "But if the concept is identical, then the interpretation ...?"

' "In principle, these are two entirely different things. The same ideas are not necessarily expressed every time by identical physical movement or vocal stress." '

In the role of Pimen Christoff evokes in us the images of those reclusive scribes of the Slavic Middle Ages, filling the parchment pages of prayer books and historical chronicles with sad confessions of their iniquities. It is worth remembering that in all these transcripts they refer to themselves as insignificant and unworthy, but behind those sombre words we can perceive not only the fear and despair but also the hidden pride of creating something worthwhile. At the beginning of the monologue in the first Act Pimen appears to be crushed by his sense of iniquity, but his secret faith in the truth and importance of the words he is writing fuels his energy and his voice quickly begins to pick up. Through the variations of the themes, which make the musical structure of this monologue so flowing, Christoff sings the words with a clear sonority, although his voice shapes the phrases intimately and quietly as though they had acquired the form of a monastic cell. The interpretation of the contrasting musical material of the part of Varlaam is performed in an entirely different way. Christoff lays bare the violent and temperamental nature of the wanderer/false monk/drunk in a lively and exuberant manner. His voice now radiates the liberated energy that he had not been able to use before.

These two roles, like the chorus, which powerfully and insistently reveals the feelings of the masses, are directly linked with the role of Boris Godunov. Christoff's interpretation recreates the role of the tragic Tsar. Popular unrest is growing and Boris Godunov is drawn into this process along with his own torments. This is revealed by his own shattered peace of mind. The uprising, the boyars' intrigues, the famine and the prayer for the murdered Tsarevich are reflected both in the songs of the masses and in Boris's monologues. Pure parental feelings and fear of retribution, love of power and repentance create a graphic reflection of the monumental struggle between the collective conscience and personal downfall and between untrammelled ambition and the hidden truth.

Christoff makes enthusiastic use of these dramatic turning points because they embody the powerful and unchangeable truth towards which Mussorgsky was striving and because through them he had the opportunity to make use of all the beautiful qualities of his voice. The free monologues introduced into the opera with such astonishing innovative confidence are in complete harmony with its broad vocal line, its ability to sustain psychological intensity and to fascinate with rhetorical expressiveness. On stage, Christoff's tonal variations are fully in accord with the internal development of Godunov's soul, with the content of the words, with his miming and the action on stage in general.

With his feeling for line he achieved a superb unity between declamation on the one hand and lyrical outpourings on the other. His anger and the subsequent suffering in the scene with Shuisky are immensely affecting. The groans of an oppressed imagination mingle with a sense of rage and fear to shape the quiet lamentation for his children: 'Lord ... you see the tears of a sinful father. I am not praying for myself....' With him these words are no longer singing but a prayer: his scarcely audible voice lends to the words a patina of purity and translucence. On this, as on many other occasions, Christoff upholds the principles of which Hegel said: 'The human voice is perceived as the sound of the soul itself' and 'In song the soul speaks from its own body'.

In the Death scene, the funeral bell announces the end. In horror Boris realizes this: 'My hour has come! God!' Christoff delivers these words with all his might. He is still Tsar and, rising up against his torments, tries to address God as an equal: 'I am still Tsar!' The crescendos are motivated in the same way as the diminuendos – and now, at the end, he has with terrifying power reached the heights of his despotic ambitions only to crash in an even more terrifying manner, to be transformed once again into a man with a dying 'Ah'. His death is as dramatic as his entire reign on stage. In every moment – in the prologue and in the recitative in the second act – he is burdened with one and the same thought and a searing conscience. That is expressed by means of contrasting musical material in tones, melodiously produced whether they are severe or tender, and at the same time always historically authentic. Perhaps it was just this that the English painter Leonard Boden had in mind when he painted Christoff as a monumental sculpture (see cover). He portrayed him against a plain background with a low horizon in a heavy costume that weighed more than 40 kilos and which had innumerable royal decorations but not a single gentle or wayward wrinkle. He painted him with a stern and manly profile. It was truly like a monument.

When he began to immerse himself in the subtleties of the Russian masterpieces of the theatre Christoff relied a great deal on Dobrowen, Sanin and Labinsky. Of course, he took up their ideas only after he had been convinced of their value; but after that he could not consider any other interpretation. He recalled that, some time at the end of the 1940s, when he created the role of Boris Godunov for the first time in a production by Sanin, in the first Act Tsar Boris Godunov began by singing softly. At one of the rehearsals, when he had already come to the conclusion that he had hit upon the right tone, Sanin told him: 'You are singing very loudly.' Since that time, when he makes his appearance in the Coronation scene he takes several steps forward with his gaze fixed on the audience; after the orchestra has died down, he places his left hand on his chest and pronounces in a solemn voice: 'My soul is sad! A secret terror haunts me; with evil presentiments my heart is filled.'

He begins very quietly, singing as if to himself: at this point in the score Mussorgsky wrote *piano*. Christoff catches the attention of the audience with this phrase, and he begins to pray: 'O Lord above, O father....' After crossing himself three times he opens his eyes and turns his gaze to the heavens. After this his voice becomes stronger, and the tension begins to increase. For him this is a decisive moment: throughout the development of the action it is, as always, a question of psychological nuance. If asked to explain these 'nuances', Christoff refers one to the score, to Pushkin's text and, of course, to his own experience. He insists that one must strictly adhere to that which the authors themselves were seeking to achieve, and that one must study and respect the context, the characters and the main trends of development in the musical drama as well as the moral conclusions to be drawn. The same treatment should be given to the so-called 'didactics' – the indications that the composer himself has written above the score. Then one will discover the right tempo, rhythm and tone for a given passage. That is the goal one should aim for. The artist must carry the spiritual development within himself. The listener must be able to hear every word.

After such an explanation he may begin to sing, to show how the musical phrase and thoughts must be linked: 'Here I reply after a long pause. What does that mean? I approach Xenia. In the pause I realize where I am. I extract from the psychological nuances my decisions, my behaviour on stage, my gestures and my tone.'

Those who have been present on such occasions realize that he is speaking not only as a singer who has studied a given score, but as a producer, a painter and a historian. Sanin taught him that Boris has to 'round up the boyars like a herd of cattle', and he tried to envisage how this would appear from every point of view. Sanin also taught him that when he sings the words 'Do not ask of me by what path I came to the throne', he should clasp his son's head to him. Experience has convinced him that this is effective. Again on Sanin's advice, he decided how he should fall from the throne in the Death scene. Sanin suggested that he should fall from on high and then be caught. In Christoff's interpretation this is a unique and powerful moment. The same might be said about his final cry. Here Mussorgsky had written *piano*, but Christoff sings it *forte*. He sings it and straight away falls. On stage Christoff's Tsar Boris personified something greater than a beautiful timbre and vocal technique: he disclosed shattering truths about crime and retribution.

The history of the second EMI recording with Christoff in 1963 is interesting. The Salle Wagram in Paris had been booked and the orchestra of the Paris Conservatoire was hired under the conductor André Cluytens. There remained the question of the chorus. Christoff suggested that the chorus of the Sofia National Opera should be invited. In May a special envoy from EMI convinced himself that the choir had great possibilities since it had a rich tradition of performing Russian operas. The inevitable dispute about the 'two versions' was decided in accordance with Christoff's views – that is, in favour of the Rimsky-Korsakov edition. On 4 September 1963 the recording began. Christoff once more sang the roles of Boris, Pimen and Varlaam – with a great sense of responsibility, and he did not hesitate to make many takes. The chorus arrived on 12 September. Everyone watched anxiously as they overcame their initial nervousness and noticed how the appearance of Christoff, who had old

As Boris Godunov, with his first
mentor, Issay Dobrowen, at La
Scala.

With Victor de Sabata at La Scala,
1950. (*Publifoto, Milan*)

During an electrifying session recording *Boris Godunov* for EMI with
André Cluytens, Paris, 1963. (*Hans Wild*)

*Top, left:* As Creonte in Cherubini's *Medea. Top, right:* As Don Basilio in *Il Barbiere di Siviglia*, Chicago, 1956. *Bottom, left:* In the title role of Rossini's *Mosè* at the 1951-2 Festival of Florence. *Bottom, right:* as Mephistophélès in Gounod's *Faust (Opera).*

*Top, left:* As Verdi's Attila in Florence, 1962. *Top, right:* As Procida in *I Vespri Siciliani*, La Scala, 1951. *Bottom, left:* As Fiesco in Verdi's *Simone Boccanegra. Bottom, right:* As Pizarro in Beethoven's *Fidelio*, 1949.

*Top:* As King Philip II in Visconti's original production of Verdi's *Don Carlos* at Covent Garden in 1958, with Tito Gobbi (*left*) as Rodrigo (*Houston Rogers/from the collections of the Theatre Museum. By courtesy of the Board of Trustees of the Victoria & Albert Museum.*) *Bottom:* Twenty-one years later as King Philip with Sylvia Sass as Elisabeth de Valois (*Reg Wilson*).

friends in the choir, electrified them. They sang 'Our folk song unites us for ever', and the atmosphere changed.

The performances by the Sofia National Opera at the San Carlo Opera House in Naples were a similar, perhaps even more brilliant page in the history of this role. They were put on at the initiative of the director of the theatre, Pascuale di Constanza, but above all to meet the wishes of the local inhabitants to see Christoff in the role of Boris Godunov. The success of the performances, the first of which was on 5 January 1970, was exceptional. Even those people who were allergic to newspaper hyperbole and the language of the music critics had something to think about when they read the headlines of the reviews of this event. They occupied two or three columns in all the principal papers published in Rome and Naples: 'Exceptional performance of Mussorgsky's Boris. A triumph for Boris Christoff – an unequalled success' (*Il Mattino* of 5 January 1970); 'Boris Christoff – supreme exponent. True success of Mussorgsky's opera with a brilliant performance by the Sofia National Opera' (*Napoli Notte* 6 January 1970).

Among the outstanding roles created by Christoff is that of Dosifey in Mussorgsky's *Khovanshchina*, which he first sang at Florence in 1949. *Khovanshchina* is a triumph of the innovative genius of Mussorgsky. In it Christoff again found magnificent opportunities to display all the colour of his vocal and dramatic range. The opera tells how the reforms of Peter the Great have wrought tragic disruption in the social and spiritual life of Russia and how the country has become entangled in a mortal struggle. In *Khovanshchina* the emphasis is not on the drama of individuals but on the head-on confrontation between conflicting groups amidst mass suffering. The populace is once again the main driving force, and in colourful groups (the Streltsy, the serf girls, and the wives of the Streltsy) they offer unusual characterization. The oppression of serfdom, the rebellious spirit, the fatalism of the Old Believers, the silhouettes of the gallows and the funeral pyres, violence and simple yearning merge into a monumental experience determined by the larger-than-life stature of the principals. Dosifey, leader of the Old Believers, is one of the most striking of these, and Christoff portrays this part superbly.

Christoff became attracted by the spiritual richness of this part when as a young man he attended a performance of *Khovanshchina* at the Sofia National Opera. Even then he could feel an affinity with those who surround Dosifey – whose role he perceived to be 'more important than that of Ivan Khovansky' (also a bass part). The final prayer of the Old Believers in the sixth scene at the end of the first act also appealed to him. It remained in his memory as one of the most beautiful scenes in all of Mussorgsky's works. 'Look at the second and third acts,' he wrote to me in a letter of 14 August 1984. 'Turn your attention to the dissent among the princes Golitsyn, Ivan Khovansky and Mishetsky (Dosifey), and you will discover even more ancient reasons for the quarrels between the first two and the true spiritual power of Dosifey. His humanity and strength are revealed in his intervention in the conversation between Marfa and Susanna (two Old Believers), one a suffering and truly loving wife, the other evil and envious.

'When Dosifey discovers the evil-doing of Susanna, I can sympathize with him when he explodes in the elemental, god-like curse: "Get thee gone, spawn of the devil!" A terrifying scene that heightens my human sensibilities. At this moment I can feel that the audience is on edge, having suddenly fallen under the lash of the Lord. Calm returns the next moment when I lift Marfa, prostrate at my feet, and she lowers her head to my shoulder and I begin to lead her from the stage, crying "… Marfa, my ailing child! Forgive me, I am the main sinner. God's will is our sorrow …". In such an analysis of my approach to Dosifey, one of my favourite heroes, one can also grasp the complexity of the ideas or knowledge on which I base my spiritual affinity with Dosifey….'

Christoff expressed similar ideas about his approach to the role of Dosifey in a letter to Assen Dimitrov on 20 April 1949: 'I have come to the conclusion that a singer must live for a long time with the characters that he portrays on stage in order to penetrate with the greatest subtlety into their external and internal life. My *Khovanshchina* opened many eyes. The depth and nature of Dosifey are so complex that at first glance it is impossible to grasp them. After 18 performances I really began to understand him. Perhaps after another 18 I began to reveal new subtleties, and who knows how many times 18 I shall need to be able to present the character as it should be played? In the striving for this sort of achievement, I find the true pleasure of our art. This is art in the true sense of the word: to know how to seek and when you have found it to know how to portray it. I can only regret that I am not near you so that I can make use of your valuable advice.'

Those who have been present at a performance of *Khovanshchina* in which Christoff took part know very well that his intentions have been fulfilled. Many reviews have been enthusiastic about these performances. The Italian critic Leonardo Pinsauti, for example, wrote: 'The Maggio Musicale Fiorentino ended this year's season with Mussorgsky's *Khovanshchina*. The overall impression of this Florentine production of *Khovanshchina* was positive because of the presence of certain singers who were capable of re-creating with astonishing immediacy the poetic ardour and dramatic vividness of some of the most complex characters in opera. Boris Christoff, who in the role of Dosifey once again displayed the power that has stirred the emotions for 25 years, had around him the Ivan Khovansky of Nicola Rossi-Lemeni and the Marfa of Amalia Pini. The world-famous bass is one of those rare artists who succeeds in becoming a "presence" the very moment he appears on stage. If one adds to this mysterious enchantment, musicality, a masterly diction and an incomparable colouring of the voice, which in the course of a lengthy career has not prevented the creation of an authentic hero, then Christoff's Dosifey continues to transmit its terrible and disturbing force.'

On 13 April 1970, Jeremy Noble wrote in *The Times*: 'This is a very difficult opera to put on because of its rather complex subject – particularly for the audience – and because of the way in which, from the dramatic point of view, the music is concentrated on quite insignificant moments. To begin with one was surprised by the fact that the Rome Opera House found it necessary to put on such a work which, despite the rich costumes and graceful decor of Nicola Benois that evoke ancient Russia, has so little interest for the Italian public, the more so since the soprano is in fact silent after the first scene. But with Boris Christoff's appearance on stage towards the end of the first act as Dosifey, the leader of the Old Believers, the entire opera receives a fresh significance and intensity. In the first place, Christoff's voice was in excellent shape and all doubts as to whether he would be able to return to his best form after his illness disappeared immediately.'

In July 1973, after Christoff had visited Budapest, *Musika* wrote: 'The role of Dosifey in Mussorgsky's *Khovanshchina* is not big, but its great weight and dramatic intensity make it all the more important. When this holy man appears, the passion and hatred among people dies down. It is the same with the boyars, who during their struggles for power submit to the personality of Dosifey. Boris Christoff was a Dosifey in which all this was credible. The great artist portrayed the father of the Orthodox with all the nobility of the prophets of the Old Testament. His singing and acting – along with his compassion – were so convincing that one felt the Old Believers listened to his words as if they were a divine revelation and were ready to follow him wherever he might lead; moreover, others respected him despite the fact that he was the personification of an old-fashioned idea. His prayer at the end of the first act was unforgettably magnificent. He gave the public moments of excitement such as they have rarely experienced. The aria in the last act represented the climax of his interpretation. Yes, his technique is perfectly secure; his *forte* is very powerful and brilliant; his *piano* is magically soft – these are the most outstanding moments of his performance. Boris Christoff is an amazing colossus of the operatic stage.'

The role of Cherevik in Mussorgsky's *Sorochintsy Fair* occupies a more modest place in Christoff's artistic biography. Musical circles in Western Europe have displayed considerably less interest in this opera, which he sang in 1959 at the Rome Opera House. The new element which he introduced into the role of Cherevik was its folklore colour. In contrast with the many-layered, dramatic and lofty images of Boris Godunov and Dosifey, Cherevik is brought to life in a fresh and lively manner in the folk-comic style of the opera as a whole. In this opera Mussorgsky re-creates a story by Gogol with animated and noisy crowd scenes, lively dances, picturesque landscapes, and his rich and precise feeling for the truth in Ukrainian life. The performance of the opera in Rome was well received. The critics wrote sparingly but with good will about Christoff's contribution. Giorgio Vigolo wrote, in *Il Matino*: 'Outstanding among the soloists was once again Boris Christoff, who in the playful comedy of Cherevik is as excellent a singer and actor as he is in the majesty of a Boris Godunov or the sublime sanctity of a Dosifey.' Another critic remarked that, so far as the cast was concerned, 'it is enough only to mention the presence of Boris Christoff to comprehend the importance of an opera of this kind. This great and very intelligent singer-actor was able once again to create the "centre" of his hero and to personify him powerfully with his vocal and acting skills.'

# 7

# *Russian Song*

Christoff's long and fruitful association with Russian classical music and Russian folk-song is closely linked to the question of the Russian language; or to be more precise the question of the connection between the word and his musical style.

Some time in July 1976, at a friend's villa near Monte Argentario, Christoff spoke to those present about the language in which he thought. He explained things simply: 'When I speak in Italian, I also think in Italian. When I speak Bulgarian, I think in Bulgarian. But do you know, once during a performance of *Boris Godunov* in London, a thought suddenly came to me in Italian. I *sang* in Italian, and became frightened. The conductor froze! I turned my back on the audience. I pulled myself together quickly and continued in Russian without the audience suspecting a thing. Naturally, Franca had realized....'

Perhaps the point is too insignificant to be worth noting.

But those who know Christoff will perceive that the episode on the stage of Covent Garden is an echo of the dramatic struggle that he waged for the 'endorsement' of the Russian language. The start came when the young Christoff proposed to the management of Covent Garden that the whole of *Boris Godunov*, along with all other Russian operas, should be performed in the original language. At that time nobody was prepared for such a suggestion and for many it came like a bolt from the blue.

The music press in Britain, Italy and the United States reported that the opposition to this proposal was strong, even fierce. To understand the significance of this reaction one must realize that nearly every European nation has waged a long struggle for the 'naturalization' of its own opera houses. Those who had set themselves the ambitious task of giving opera roots in their own soil resolutely opposed the thesis that Italian is the only language suitable for vocal performances. *Pastorale* by the poet Pierre Perrin and the musician Robert Cambert, performed in 1659, proved that French is also a 'vocal' language. The great achievements of Henry Purcell (1659–95) in the development of English musical culture was facilitated by the introduction of the English language; that is, by the realization that opera in England could find its own course only if it drew on local cultural traditions.

In fact this evolution has its local echoes in the history of Covent Garden. Despite the fact that Purcell gave English opera significance, his work had few successors. In the 19th century the English public considered itself to be cosmopolitan; many of the operas staged in England were sung by foreign artists in Italian and other languages. After the Second World War, however, the idea of translating foreign operas began to take hold when a resident company was formed in 1946 at Covent Garden: the idea, in fact, was transformed into policy. Almost all operas were now given in English. It was hoped that this reform would enable English composers, librettists and singers to make their contribution to international musical life. When Christoff proposed that Russian operas should be sung at Covent Garden in the original, he was undermining that concept.

An argument began in the press and some of the participants wrote that the suggestion was unacceptable even from a practical point of view. They believed that it would be easier and more sensible for one individual (Christoff) to learn his role in English (which he in fact knew) than to torture all the chorus and soloists with a language they did not know. They thought that the time which he had 'wasted' in disputes with the management of Covent Garden would have been quite sufficient to have achieved this. Moreover, they foresaw that the London public, which did not know Russian, would have difficulty in following what was happening on stage. Some people suggested making a translation of the libretto, which was seen as a compromise.

Martin Cooper wrote in the *Daily Telegraph* that 'the public is not interested in every phrase ... it is sufficient for them to know that Amneris is jealous ... jealousy has a limited range of expression and every one is free to imagine it according to his own taste and temperament'. Behind the arguments, however, lay wounded feelings and the unpredictable behaviour of the stars who would eventually be invited to take part in these performances. Students of history even pointed out that in the 1913–14 season the Russian Opera and Ballet visited London and performed *Boris Godunov* in Russian at Drury Lane, and that in 1928–9 Chaliapin sang the Tsar at Covent Garden in Russian while the rest of the cast sang their roles in Italian. On the latter occasion opinions were divided on the performance. If in the final analysis the dispute was settled positively, it was because those involved had to take into account Christoff's personal and general tastes and views as well as his prestige and original ideas. These ideas were worthy of attention.

Christoff stressed that one had to bear in mind the musical sound of the words; in other words, to take as one's starting point the original connection between the libretto and music for which the composer was striving. In a translation, whatever its qualities, the altered sound and structure of the language in general and individual words or phrases in particular often seem to 'go against' the music. When it comes to Mussorgsky matters become even more complicated because his innovative predilection for the original folk-language cannot be correctly learnt or understood out of context. Moreover, in Christoff's opinion some European languages are 'vocal' and others are not. He believes that Italian and Russian are the most vocal, while for phonetic reasons French, German and English cannot perform the same task. It is for that reason he is reluctant to sing his roles in translation.

Naturally one could take issue with this opinion – and not only from the point of view of injured national pride. In practice, however, it transpired that his views were eventually accepted even by those who had at first rejected them. In the autumn of 1958 numerous influential European newspapers reported that *Boris Godunov* had been performed at Covent Garden entirely in Russian for the first time. As if summing up a dispute which had been conducted with such passion and mutually exclusive arguments, the Milan newspaper *Corriere della Sera* reported: 'Boris Christoff gets his own way.'

The effect of the change of policy had been eagerly anticipated; on the day following the first night the reaction was like an explosion. The critics went into great detail noting that the chorus and the other principal singers had in only a few months achieved 'a miraculous approximation to the Russian accent'. Certain writers did not conceal their reservations and revealed that 'the difficulties of singing in Russian were audible'; but the general tone of the reviews of this enormous success was enthusiastic. The *Daily Mail* wrote that 'the eternal dispute about whether language plays an important part in the performance of a certain opera has been decisively settled'.

Echoes of this performance quickly reached the United States and on 2 November 1958 the *New York Times* reported it as a significant event. Having noted that the entire opera had been sung in Russian, the paper mentioned that the 'glittering audience at the first night warmly applauded the performers' and that the royal box was occupied by the British Prime Minister, Harold Macmillan, and the Soviet ambassador, Yakob Malik. Some days later Queen Elizabeth attended a performance of *Boris Godunov* at Covent Garden. At the end of the second act she expressed a wish to congratulate Christoff. The Queen asked him whether he was satisfied with the outcome and received the reply: 'Splendidly.'

The overwhelming opinion was that Covent Garden had had an indisputable success. Christoff sang in Russian in San Francisco, New Orleans and Chicago and at the Colon in Buenos Aires, and many people were grateful to him. Specialists continued to reflect on the results of the reform and some of them discovered, as if it were a revelation, that even when they were listening to Russian, which they did not understand, they began to comprehend its significance

and beauty, and that Christoff's pronunciation, in which the
words were shaped to the music, took precedence over the
song and was a musical delight.

In February 1979 he sang in Cologne. The hall fell silent
because the words which 'take precedence over the song'
contained impulses and insights that overcame the audience.
Christoff wrote in his album devoted to Mussorgsky that the
song 'The Winds are Howling', written on 28 March 1864 to
words by A. Koltsov, is enriched by themes and tonalities
from Russian folklore and that in it the composer is seeking
an even clearer individual sound. That is how the song
sounds in Christoff's perceptive performance, which
contains the 'complete unification of the syllable with
musical perfection', as Guido Pannain put it.

Between 1955 and 1957 Christoff was able to realize one of
the great ambitions of his career – the recording of 63 songs
by Mussorgsky (on four records) and the printing of a book
of notes for the album. The recording was made by HMV in
Paris, with the pianist Alexandre Labinsky. The text was
printed in Paris on 30 June 1958. Christoff made the
selection, wrote the detailed analysis of every song, and
organized the translations into various languages (every song
was printed in Russian, English, French and Italian). The
critics accurately described this achievement as pioneering.
But when the project had been completed, when the
questions connected with the scores, the translations, the
printing, the proof-reading and the search for the truest style
had all been settled, scarcely anyone was interested in the
problems involved in creating the set (see Discography).

Guido Pannain, Joseph Kessel and Vladimir Feodorov
contributed articles to the album's booklet. The first wrote a
superb analysis of Mussorgsky's work and did not fail to note

that in his opinion Christoff had made an exceptional contribution to the popularization of these works after the Second World War. In this article as in many other publications he put forward the view that in Mussorgsky's songs 'Boris Christoff has penetrated right into their being and into their lyric intensity. The fact that we have become acquainted with these songs is entirely due to him.' After this introduction, Joseph Kessel surveyed the life and times of the composer, and Vladimir Feodorov paid particular attention to the manuscript of 18 songs by Mussorgsky which had found their way to France and in 1911 entered the library of the Paris Conservatoire. It is assumed that these songs, with the overall title *The Youthful Years, A Collection of Romances*, had been prepared by the composer himself, either for publication or to display his work abroad, and had probably left Russia with some singer who intended to perform them in France. Some of the songs were reminiscent of, or improved versions of, material written on other occasions. Despite the fact that they contained nothing sensational or shocking, the publication of the album itself did cause a sensation.

Those who produced the set and those who later wrote reviews in the press about it did not have to plead for attention from anyone. They knew that it was a great work which would win over many to Mussorgsky's songs, and so they indulged their right to be able to enjoy it first. Christoff himself placed the dedication in the introduction: 'In memory of my brother Nikolai. Boris Christoff. It was profound admiration for the genius of Modeste Mussorgsky that induced me to devote myself to the art of singing; and thus the whole course of my life was changed, for previously I had planned on a career in law. The new artistic horizons that the discovery of Mussorgsky's music revealed led me to establish myself in Italy – where all arts are born – and here I was able to develop as man and artist. In this favourable atmosphere I consecrated myself entirely to music. Later I made several appearances in France, where my interpretation of Russian music won prompt recognition. These successes aroused the desire of making a complete recording of Mussorgsky's melodies, and I am grateful to His Master's Voice for having given me the opportunity of realizing this recording with the valuable collaboration of M. René Challan.

'I have adopted a chronological order so as to give a clearer picture of the development of his art. But here I must state that it is wrong to divide the life of Mussorgsky into periods of progress and decline. From the very first moment his creativity maintained a very high level. It is true that a deep understanding of this composer's music requires a knowledge of his life, since the connection between his life and art is so close and indivisible. All his compositions are inspired by real events and emotions. That is why I wrote a commentary on each of the songs, the aim of which is to be useful to the listener without resort to technical terminology.

'I have devoted many years to studying the problem of interpreting the music of Mussorgsky. I have studied his thoughts and his life in order to penetrate more deeply into his art. The sense of release I felt when I sang the melodies, romances and scenes accorded with his style.

'*Songs and Dances of Death*, *The Winds are Howling* and *The Song of Mephistopheles* had been conceived by the author for orchestra but had not been thus performed. I preferred to make use of the orchestrations by Rimsky-Korsakov, Glazunov and Labinsky so as to preserve the wealth of their colour.'

The first song in the album is 'Where are you, little star?':

> Where are you, bright little star?
> Are you covered by a black cloud,
> A black cloud, a gloomy cloud?
> Where are you, beautiful maiden?
> Have you left your dear friend,
> Your dear friend, your beloved?
> The black cloud has hidden the little star,
> The cold ground has taken the maiden.

In his notes for the song Boris Christoff wrote: 'A Romance for voice and piano. Written in 1857 in St Petersburg to a text presumed to be by Mussorgsky himself, written in the spirit of folk song. Dedicated to I.L. Gryunberg. First published in 1911. The manuscript is in Paris (Library of the Conservatoire). This is Mussorgsky's first composition for voice and piano. He was 18 years of age at the time. Still inexperienced as a composer, he was guided by his sound musical intuition. Before this, he had turned his attention to folk melodies in the Phrygian mode, which was sometimes used in Russian folk music. Without doubt Mussorgsky had intended to orchestrate the song, since in the manuscript before the theme of the introduction he had noted "*dudka*" (cor anglais). The melody has a free rhythm, especially at the beginning, and is reminiscent of the improvisation of folk singers. Its romantic and melancholic tone predicts the future personality of the composer, who was to become a matchless bard of human melancholy.' In these concise and convincing descriptions, Christoff showed his artistic and musical appreciation of this song. The preparations for recording the song were completed on the 100th anniversary of its composition.

In the song anguish is veiled like a hidden and melancholy

lament for the dead maiden. Solitude seeks an answer –
'Where are you, little star?' Christoff's warm voice seems to
sink to the ground, weighed down by the burden of sorrow.
It descends low and evenly over the steppes, after which it
momentarily rediscovers its energy and soars upward
towards the sky. But the little star is not there. The lonely
one is met by a dark cloud, a black and gloomy cloud. The
voice of sorrow once again descends to the depths, merging
with its own echo from the upper air. But the beautiful young
maiden is not here either. The voice grows stronger as if trying
to recreate and depict the beloved. Alas, this is but a dream.
Above hangs the dark cloud. Once again the voice soars
towards the cloud, passionate and powerful, as if trying to
disperse it with its deep anguish. Then it falls, finally despair-
ing – the cloud has concealed the little star and the cold earth
has swallowed up the maiden....

In the album the subsequent 30 songs are arranged in
chronological order. So far as themes and musical inspiration
are concerned they are all quite distinct, so that when one
listens to them one experiences a variety of emotions, mir-
roring from different angles the ideals and images Mussorgsky
has preserved in his heart. Christoff compels the listener to
look within himself because the essence of what he is singing
lies not only in the story but in the melancholy or tender
lyricism that merges into the themes evoking the landscape.
He discloses picturesque visions which are pure and weightless; later, he draws them towards himself with magical
insight into the melodies with his stress on various syllables
and phrases, or pours them forth like sighs, like fiery weeping
in the night or like scalding tears. In some songs these rich
images, which Christoff's voice conjures with such complex
and picturesque nuances, are replaced by comic situations or
cheerful laughter which clearly reflect the musical style.

'Night', by Pushkin, creates a particularly powerful impression:

> My voice caressing and languorous for you
> Disturbs the silence of the black night,
> My sad candle by my bed
> Burns. My words, slurring and murmuring,
> Flow, a stream of love, full, so full of you!
> In the black night your eyes flash before me,
> They smile at me and I hear sounds!
> My friend, my dear friend, I love you....

In his notes to the album Christoff wrote of this song: 'Written on April 10, 1864, in St Petersburg, to a text by Pushkin. Dedicated to Nadezhda P. Opochinina.... Mussorgsky left two versions of this work. The first is based on a text by Pushkin, while the second is based on the same text but rewritten by Mussorgsky in rhythmical prose. His text does not have the elegance of Pushkin's version, but the music is of a high quality, since Mussorgsky expresses the meaning of the words in the character of the music. The connection of thought, words and music is for him not just a theory but a creative necessity. He eliminated some real blemishes from Pushkin's poetry, and drew a pure and mystical portrait of a beloved woman in an idealized and platonic form. Mussorgsky orchestrated this song in 1868, but only a few bars from this orchestration are preserved in the State Library in Leningrad. The manuscript in Paris differs in both music and text from that in Leningrad.'

Something else can be grasped from the interpretation of 'Night'. Few songs present such a pure and charming image of a lover's yearnings, and here Mussorgsky is deeply indebted to Christoff's interpretation. Did not Shakespeare call music 'the food of love' and did not Wagner add that 'one cannot see the essence of music in anything other than love'? Christoff's voice confirms this. With vigorous modulations he dissolves into streams of love and becomes intoxicated with happiness and the strength of his feelings. His imagination speeds into the night (the final lines are the exact text by Pushkin), but when he perceives the flashing eyes of his beloved in the darkness his outpourings fall silent. His tone expresses expectation, desire and even breathlessness. It dies down before the flashing eyes, becomes hushed as if it is not singing but is listening to its own echo and becomes tender and caressing with the words 'yours, yours'. Although his inimitable *mezza voce* is to be found in most of the songs in this album, some critics have specifically referred to it in this song. Christoff himself considers this song to be the composer's masterpiece.

Seven of Mussorgsky's songs comprise the *Nursery* cycle. Christoff showed the same interest in them, because he realized that the composer had immersed himself in them not to seek relief from the torments of his conscience but rather to take a fresh look at Russian folk art in the light of happy recollections of his childhood. These songs are coloured by children's whimsical curiosity, and by the fears, innocent ideas and inspiration of fairy stories and folklore. Mussorgsky himself sang them to his brother's children and their friends, and said: 'This is the best audience that has ever heard me sing!' Perhaps Christoff felt a special affinity with them because he has in his art collection the original drawing by Repin for the first edition in 1872. When he looks at this drawing on the walls of his study, he feels the need to shape every performance anew so as to make his listeners aware of the same delights, as if for the very first time.

A central place in Mussorgsky's songs is occupied by the

cycles *Sunless* and *Songs and Dances of Death*. Christoff wrote of the first songs of *Sunless*: 'A cycle of songs for voice and piano composed in 1874 in St Petersburg to a text by Count A.A. Golenishchev-Kutuzov. Mussorgsky's brief stay on earth is full of experiences that often assume a tragic nature. While he was still young he was grief-stricken at the death of a girl he loved, and later by the death of his mother, whom he adored. The loss of people who were close to him, financial difficulties and the need to waste valuable time in low-ranking state service had a powerful effect on his delicate and sensitive nature.... Aware of the spiritual fortitude necessary to combat his enemies, who were also enemies of the new movement and of his friends, he was the standard-bearer of the new ideal and was always the first in the struggle. He withstood the blows.... But there was one thing he could not bear: disloyalty between himself and his true friends, with whom he had formed the neo-Russian school and with whom he laid down fresh rules for musical truth. Dargomyzhsky was dead, true to his beliefs, but others of his beloved friends were spiritually dead because they had one after another deserted their basic principles. Now he was abandoned by his friends and by the society in which he had grown up, physically exhausted and morally shattered.

'This mental state also influenced his friend and relative Arseny Golenishchev-Kutuzov, a young poet, for whom Mussorgsky felt a pure love and in whom he confided during the time they shared an apartment. Kutuzov's verse *Sunless* arose from this mental state and Mussorgsky set it to outstanding music as a reflection of his desperate solitude.'

The notes for *Songs and Dances of Death* are similar: 'A cycle of songs for voice and piano; Mussorgsky intended to orchestrate them but they were orchestrated after his death by Glazunov and Rimsky-Korsakov to a text by Count

Golenishchev-Kutuzov. [The critic] Stassov considers that his own contribution was to give Mussorgsky the idea for this cycle. But Stassov insisted that the composition of *Dances of Death* was based on a subject taken from history, and that he tried to convince Golenishchev-Kutuzov of this rather than Mussorgsky. The truth is, however, different. The events and principles by which Mussorgsky shaped his career, from the first creative years, in all aspects of his life, aided him in the composition of his music. Death was the theme of one of his first songs, inspired by an especially dramatic moment in *Boris Godunov.* He knew Liszt's *Danse Macabre* and thought highly of his work; he knew Schubert's *Erlkönig,* and *Death and the Maiden* as well as Berlioz's *Dies Irae.* But he wanted to create something else. He wished to portray death according to his own philosophical concepts, and he found the answer in the moving lyrics of Golenishchev-Kutuzov. Just as in *Boris Godunov,* Mussorgsky succeeded in portraying with impressive dramatic power the struggle between man and death in the 'Lullaby' from *Songs and Dances of Death.* The four songs are divided into two parts: in the first Mussorgsky describes the scene of the action and the participants, in the second (or monologue) he depicts death with hatred.... He was not an atheist, but it is certain that by the end of his life he had become a profound pessimist....'

Christoff makes a connection between the songs and specific events in Mussorgsky's life. He links them with his disappointments, with Stassov's letters and with the views of his enemies. He knew quite well, however, that the two song cycles did not simply reflect a painful personal state, but dealt with a drama on a broader social and psychological scale; he knew, too, that they were expressed in the authentic form and sound of the living Russian folk music. Mussorgsky tried to imbue them with a 'generalized', all-embracing sound, making use of every opportunity for programmatic association based on their literary sources. It is no coincidence that the record notes include reproductions of details of Repin's *Boyarka Morozova* and the *Way of the Cross in Kursk Gubernia*, showing images of cripples and hunchbacks. Inspired by these and dozens of other similar images, by thoughts and concerns from his peripatetic and varied youth, and by ideas from Russian literature, he shaped and coloured each of the songs.

The manner in which Christoff dealt with country themes in these recordings is an exceptional achievement. Mussorgsky saw in the classics of Russian literature, as well as the songs he himself composed, the reincarnation of his native land indissolubly linked with the fate of the people inhabiting it. He transferred social and moral problems to the heavens among the clouds and the stars, to the steppes where the stormy winds blow, and to the woods where the leaves rustled mournfully. He did so not to conceal them from people's gaze but, by means of these associations, to give them a tragic universality. The harmonies, typical of him, and the free variations he employed, help to make these associations direct and almost palpable.

Christoff's approach helped greatly to achieve Mussorgsky's intentions through his emotional and vocal colouring. He placed his trust in Nature, and portrayed it not as a background or a milieu but as a heightened form of existence. His voice becomes magically transformed into an echo that weeps in the cold, or into a passionate storm through which man's grief penetrates the whole of the material world around him. In his interpretations the musical moods and tones are directly linked with visual images. There, as we listen to him, we can see and feel nature. With the pictorial, tinted and textured characteristics of his musical language we are able to visualize all those new elements that appeared in Russian landscape painting in the very years when Mussorgsky was composing his songs. In the second half of the 19th century the visionaries affirmed that natural ideas were inseparable from the social and critical ideas of the time.

Christoff has no difficulty with pictorial representation because his own ideas are in complete accord with the harmonic, instrumental-tonal colouring of Mussorgsky. They are always clear, yet at the same time remote, mystical and equivocal, just as the literary originals are: sounds echo dejectedly; somewhere in the distance crowds of people disperse in the gloom; the room is sunk in impenetrable darkness; the harbinger-star flickers behind the clouds....

The link between the general and the specific is particularly vivid in 'Trepak' from *Songs and Dances of Death*:

> The deserted forest and glades lie all around,
> The snowstorm weeps and moans,
> It seems as if in the nocturnal gloom,
> Someone is being buried;
> Look, it is so! In the darkness music
> Embraces death, caresses,
> And dances the trepak with the drunkard.
> The song rings in the ear:
> Oh, wretched old man,
> You got yourself drunk, trudged along the road,
> But the snowstorm, the witch, arose, played with you,
> Drove you from the field into the dense unknown
>     forest.
> My darling, I shall warm you with the snow,
> Sleep, my friend, my happy man,
> Spring has come, nature is blooming!

The sun smiles over the cornfield.
A song can be heard and the doves are flying....

In his interpretation of this song, as on many other
occasions, Christoff as it were draws his voice directly from
the majesty and mysteries of nature: his timbre sounds like a
many-voiced echo of the things that the forests, glades,
deserts and winter wind say about themselves. They are
disturbing since one senses that in the nocturnal gloom 'evil
death is burying someone'. The feeling is not mistaken:
Death really is leading the drunken peasant along unknown
paths. The song's rhythm and tension change. Christoff
'approaches', so as to observe this terrible dance close at
hand. Death sings in the ear of its victim, and resounds
throughout the deserted countryside. Hastily and breathless-
ly it showers him with cynical promises, envelops him in
the veil of the snowstorm and begins to relate to him its
terrible tale. Later it rises as loud and as hurried as the storm
itself in order to collect the clouds, the woods and the flying
snow so as to cover the unfortunate peasant for ever. Then,
after the crime has been committed, the voice once again
returns to the present day. Christoff now pronounces the
words tenderly because what has just happened is real, and
he sings of the summer and the sun which will once again
warm the spirits. He sings once again like the echo of what
nature is saying about itself and is borne upwards like the
wing of a bird, like the silence in which 'the doves are flying'.
Immediately after the appearance of the album its
significance was discussed in print. Critics were excited and
delighted by Christoff's complete identity with Mussorgsky's songs and by the unexpectedly complex and
touching sound of the whole recording. Some of them began
to wonder if Mussorgsky was indeed revealed most

convincingly in *Boris Godunov* and *Khovanshchina* or if his genius and innovative power was not more magnificently displayed in these simple little songs. Teodoro Celli wrote: 'The complete recording of Mussorgsky's songs issued by La Voix de son Maître is the true monument to his memory.... Christoff's voice possesses the touch, impregnated with melancholy, that we feel to be the singular talent of the Slavs. His voice is full of stormy outbursts and yet is capable of yielding to resignation.... I consider that Mussorgsky's greatest work is not *Boris Godunov*, but the songs on these four discs that contain the secret of his musical drama.' Other experts and musicologists discussed this 'monument' in Italy, England and France. Their high opinions were shaped by an understanding of just how difficult it is to perform these songs and of the mastery Christoff had displayed in doing so. What dark tenderness there was in his voice, what breadth in his vocal line, and what astonishing sensitivity and taste in his tonal nuances.

In September 1958 the reviewer in *Le Figaro* wrote: 'Pathé-Marconi has issued an outstanding work – a recording of all 63 of Mussorgsky's songs sung by Boris Christoff.... Mussorgsky is wonderful and a genius, without weaknesses and clichés. The singer, Christoff, is incomparable! What other artist has such ability and such a rich vocal range? The set contains strength, tears, vitriolic laughter, a peasant voice, suppressed weeping and a childish whisper.' In June 1959, *Messagero di Roma* carried a review that did not agree with the strict chronological order in which the songs had been placed, but immediately added that 'this is only a minor point and, thanks to the exceptional beauty and nobility of these songs and their interpretation, Mussorgsky has at last been restored to his place as the father of a style which is bound to have the maximum influence on the whole of modern music.' *Corriere della Sera*, in March 1959, asserted that 'We are no longer dealing with the Holy Russia of a tormented tsar, but with that mysterious Russia in which the spirits and demons of Dostoyevsky roam and in which the beloved springs of Tolstoy bloom ... An intimate Russia, a mighty Russia of the 19th century which lives and speaks through the most inspired pages of its literature.' [This collection is now available on CD. See Discography.]

During the 25 years which followed Christoff continued to work with inspiration on these songs, always seeking something greater than what he had already committed to record. He 're-created' this album in dozens of concert halls throughout the world. Those who had described the album as a 'monument to Mussorgsky' had long been vindicated, but every new concert performance of the songs by Christoff gave them reason to feel enriched. The enthusiastic tone in their reviews had not diminished. In June 1973, more than 15 years after the appearance of the album, *The Guardian* wrote about a concert Christoff gave in Aldeburgh (Suffolk): on 1 June: 'Last night's recital by Boris Christoff, accompanied by Nikita Magaloff, for the most part consisted of a collection of Mussorgsky's sad songs, including *Sunless* and *Songs and Dances of Death*. If to begin with some were disappointed at the great Bulgarian bass's choice, subsequently it transpired that these songs, songs of black contrast, were performed with intensity and intimacy....' The *Daily Telegraph* wrote of the same recital: 'On the podium the singer created the intensity of disturbing emotions and gloom, achieved with an hypnotic effect, thanks to the manner in which he interpreted the songs – with his eyes closed, with clenched fists, as if the artist himself was living out his art on stage....'

These recordings were only part of Christoff's creative

plan to master the glory of Russian music. Also for EMI he recorded works by the other members of the 'Mighty Handful': Balakirev, Cui, Borodin and Rimsky-Korsakov. What united them was more important for him than that which would later divide them. What was more important was their common innovative approach to form, their love of Russian folk music and their ambition to invigorate their native musical culture with original sounds and 'picturesque-romantic' emphases. In Christoff's view they were united as the 'Balakirev circle', as Vasily Stassov had affirmed at the time. He selected songs from various stages of their development, but in every case he tried to demonstrate their common creative concerns. This is why, in the notes to the Mussorgsky album, their portraits are shown together, grouped around Repin's painting of Stassov.

Fourteen songs were recorded for the disc devoted to Mily Balakirev (1837–1910). Christoff has a good understanding of the role this composer played in the folkloric, innovative national movement in Russian musical life of the 1860s. He also knows why the other members of the 'Mighty Handful' recognized him as leader. He recalls the words of Rimsky-Korsakov: 'We listened to him intently because we had a great admiration for him personally. Young, with marvellous, mobile and fiery eyes, with a fine beard, he spoke decisively, authoritatively and frankly and he was prepared at any moment to improvise at the piano.... He exuded charm like no other person. Appreciative of the slightest sign of talent in others, he was unable to perceive his own superiority over them.'

Since he envisaged Balakirev precisely like this – with 'enormous charm', 'fiery eyes' and a rare temperament and will-power – Christoff selected from his romances and Russian folk-song adaptations those songs with the most disturbing psychological preoccupations, the brightest picturesque-romantic inspiration and the most complex, tragic range of feelings. He seems to have discovered in them something of his own temperament and feelings; or, rather, something of his own conception of the role of moral energy in the creative process. It is significant that the cycle which he loves most begins with 'Intonation': a song which sounds like a manifesto for the abolition of serfdom over the Russian song, a song which calls for the liberation of folk culture from the chains that bind it, a song reverberating with the significance of the events of 1861:

> Oh, it is time for you to be free, Russian song,
> Ringing, victorious, expansive,
> Noble, of the settlements, on the outskirts,
> Beset by bad weather and misfortune.
> Bathed in blood, in blood, in peasants' tears....
> Oh, it is time for you to be free, Russian song.
> You did not only sing of yourself as you lay down.
> You were covered with snow and rain from the waste
>     land,
> You were covered with smoke and soot from the fires,
> The snowstorm drifted over you from the damp graves.

Christoff's interpretation captures the mood and the sentiment exactly. With his broad vocal line he expresses his feelings powerfully, releasing them to take possession of the expanses, without any restraint. Serfdom has already been abolished. His voice raises the song of liberation and it shines with true nobility.

'The Song of Selim', which exemplifies the connections between Balakirev's and Glinka's music, contains reflections of romantic wanderings through the lands of the Orient. Its themes, reflecting the landscape and a passionate appeal to a

maiden, denote a sharp change of mood. The moon floats
serenely in the sky, but the words directed at the young man
are bewitching:

> The moon floats,
> Quiet and serene.
> But the young soldier
> Is going off to the fight.
> Be faithful to the Prophet,
> But more faithful to love!
> He who betrays love,
> With bloody treachery,
> Without striking down the foe,
> Will die ingloriously.

Christoff faithfully interprets the rich associations in
Mikhail Lermontov's text, but at the beginning he pays
attention to Balakirev's march rhythm, not to the themes
expressing the picturesque. The moon also moves to a march
rhythm, just like the young man going off to war. The
maiden's voice sounds the same – not tender and murmuring
but clear and imperative. It sounds energetic and loud, as if
there was no one else in the world but he who had been
summoned by war, who had to be true to the calls: 'Be
faithful to the Prophet', 'Be faithful to love'. After this
injunction has been pronounced the moon appears again,
but now it truly is 'quiet and serene'. And here Christoff's
voice has already become shrouded in mist under the dome
of the heavens.

Another of the romances which makes a sharp impression
is 'The Desert' with words by Zhemchuzhnikov. This also
contains contrasts between natural and psychological
situations – the real one involving a desert from which a man
emerges exhausted, and the dream of the green garden to

which he is transported in his thoughts. Christoff is directly involved in both but he interprets them with different nuances in his tone. In the first he struggles painfully through the sands and truly suffers from the silence and the parched infinity: his voice is of the earth and full of the scorched hues of the desert. Later his thoughts carry him ahead, far beyond the steppe, to the cool garden, which, alas! he does not know if he will ever reach. This spiritualism is a salvation – at least for the spirit which has gone ahead. It sounds like resignation, even like a farewell (' … and I shall rest and forget for ever … '). The listener becomes involved not just with the direct interpretation of the text and with its vocal expression, but also with the hidden themes in the argument and with the metaphors of contrast.

So it was that all these songs, which are little known in Western Europe, all these exciting revelations of Russian poetic and vocal genius, were reincarnated thanks to Christoff. He had warmed with his feelings the rebellious seeds of the 'Mighty Handful' and they prospered. As one critic wrote, Christoff's voice, trembling with emotion, 'ran the whole range of melodic colouring, revealing emotions with tempestuous directness, sometimes with a fiery vitality that occasionally turned into bravado, on other occasions with an elevated and devotional concentration or with a velvety sweetness.'

One evening Boris Christoff returned to the subject of his beloved Russian songs. We were in his room in Bertoloni Street in Rome with two other people – a painter and an art dealer. We had been to a trattoria near the Tiber. It was quite natural that, after having heard the voice of Christoff in the theatre or over the air, the two others should harbour hopes of hearing something from Christoff's repertoire. Without much prompting he quietly intoned some ancient

Russian melodies and then went to his records. He removed
the crown of Verdi's King Philip II and set off like one of
Gorky's vagabonds from the Russian steppes as if he had
anticipated this moment with bitterness and hope in his
heart. The records changed but the repertoire remained the
same and the gramophone was played at full volume. For
him it was as if this was a convenient and long-awaited
opportunity to tell us something very valuable. He wanted
to reveal everything to us before we left. I have heard him
speak many times, with his words coming directly from the
heart, revealing how very attached he is to Russian music,
but I had never before heard him to be so categorical: 'Now
listen to my beloved "Nochenka" (Little Night)! This is my
ideal. It has always been my icon of human inspiration.'

At first I could not grasp the full significance of this
statement. Did he really prefer 'Nochenka' to Philip II's
monologue or the death throes of Boris Godunov? Did this
popular folk song reveal more brilliance and depth than the
church music of Chesnokov, Strumsky, Tchaikovsky or
Dobri Christoff? He, however, gently turned the record over
and delicately insisted that we should listen to it closely,
especially that last bar. And we listened. 'Ah, you,
nochenka ...'. He forced us to love this 'Nochenka', to
immerse ourselves in it, thrilled, as if we were weightless in
the darkness. He forced us to believe in it, bewitched by the
solitude that the fairy-tale gloom had bestowed upon us.
This sensation, which transfixed us like all great art and
which made us more unworldly, was truly spiritual. When
we left it was already getting light outside but for a long time
we remained in the embrace of that gentle and dark
'Nochenka'.

On other occasions I had the good fortune to hear
Christoff's views on the wealth of Russian music and his

spiritual commitment to it. Sometimes the conversations led in this direction by chance – for example, when we were discussing Issay Dobrowen. Nevertheless, what he said sounded like a firm conviction. Always on these occasions it was as if the main topic had been forgotten in order to leave one abiding thought which could be transformed into tears, anger and happiness.

'Once, a good friend gave me a collection of songs by Bortnyansky dating from around 1790. Marvellous. To see how that man took contemporary Western music and clothed it with Slavonic sensibility. It is simply amazing! I did not know all of these songs but among them there was some church music I had sung. But some of his songs should be better known since they soothe man's feelings. He studied in Italy under Baldassare Galuppi, and he is one of the most perceptive composers, capable of moving his listeners with a gentle spiritual lament.'

Dmitry Stepanovich Bortnyansky, little known in the West, is written about in every comprehensive history of Russian music, and not only because he wrote chamber music, operas, piano sonatas and instrumental and vocal ensembles. His ten years in Italy enabled him to achieve in his operas a noble elegance, grace and pure stylistic line which was a significant advance on the vocal-vaudeville style of Russian opera in the 18th century. It is also known that he had a real influence on Russian church music right up to the second half of the 19th century. Christoff obviously wanted him to be remembered.

Christoff would sometimes raise the subject of Russian song in a pause in conversation or because of some thought that had come to him and he embellished it with his own personal feelings: 'Mussorgsky and Rimsky-Korsakov shared a room for two years: one was working on the second version of *Boris Godunov* and the other on *The Maid of Pskov*, and they were happy. That was something exceptional. Later Mussorgsky left and wrote his songs. In one a young boy is walking along, a simple-minded young man who expresses his love ('Savishna'). His friend Cesar Cui seriously criticized the tempi: 'What singer is capable of performing these songs?' Cui offended his friend and it is from that time the tension between the two began. When they parted, Borodin said: "Understand – this is logical! When we were chicks, we lived in the same nest. We have now learnt how to fly and each of us is trying to fly along his own path." '

Christoff drew no conclusions from these stories – he was simply happy to express out loud something which had reminded him of his working years. If anyone seated at the table tried to follow up these thoughts, he was unlucky. The next moment Christoff might turn his gaze to a fishing boat on the nearby Tiber and exclaim with the same enthusiasm: 'Look at that boat. They are fishing and no doubt they have wine with them.... I do not like hunting – I simply cannot shoot animals. But fishing is something else. How we used to get soaked on the river Iskar....'

I can recall other unusual occasions. One evening in the Bulgarian embassy in Rome, when all those present were beginning to leave, Christoff unexpectedly began to sing. In front of the door to the oval marbled hall, under the baroque platform, he barred the way, turned to his wife, Franca, and began to sing an old Russian song:

> Where are you, my happiness?
> Where are you, my life? I know you have gone without me.
> It is already time to know.
> I shall no longer see you.
> Ah, night, ah, little night, ah!
> Ah, I cannot sleep.

I alone know why
You, my girl, you alone
Disturb me.


Some of those present knew this song: it was not the first time that he had sung it. But even those Italians who had not heard it before, or did not know Russian, surely perceived its meaning and sweetness. He was singing the song of a Russian exile written some time in the 17th century, the words of which lead one along a path of suffering to which there is perhaps no end. I imagined that this song took one across a boundless plain. I knew that it had drawn others along similar distant, bleak and difficult paths. After the song had ended everyone was silent: there was nothing for us to say.

Some time in June 1977, this time in the Rome apartment of some Bulgarians, Christoff once again gave proof that Russian music in the 18th and 19th centuries had created 'some wonderful things'. A group of young art students from Sofia were listening to him for the first time and could scarcely have imagined that the topic of the Russian folk song would be raised so forcefully. As might be expected, it was not long before his records were on the gramophone, but he showed no interest in them. At one moment, however, as if he had thought of something, he said he wished to hear Psalm 137 and the prayer of St Simeon and gave a long commentary on them: 'That great and holy melody really is a prayer.'

Later, just as unexpectedly, he put on a recording of a Roman vocal and instrumental trio (Count Poshka, Valentina Ponomaryeva and Georgi Kvik) and played it several times. It replaced everything else, to the great surprise of everyone, and Christoff said: 'They sing marvellously. That is a great tradition. Do you know, I do not like "open" voices. It is a shame when beautiful prayers are sung without insight. And they sing marvellously.'

As he smiled there was no sign of affectation on his face. He smiled openly and intimately as if he were prepared to share his life with those people, and he showed that he was not prepared to talk about anything else.

At a concert in the Santa Cecilia Academy on 25 February 1977, Christoff performed songs by Marco da Gagliano, Leonardo Leo, Luigi Rossi and Alessandro Stradella, little-known Italian composers of the baroque era and also by Handel and Schubert. He included in the recital six songs by Rachmaninov and Rimsky-Korsakov. This programme was difficult to perform. One might add that it was also moving – at least so far as its excellent execution was concerned. But when the enthusiastic audience rose to its feet, he responded with one old Russian folk song and one song by Mussorgsky. Nobody was surprised at this. As always, of course, the works for the inevitable encores had been prepared in advance, but this changed nothing. In the press on the following day, just as at the concert itself, his performance of the Russian song was perceived as an event. The audience had seen something fresh and truly significant in his interpretation, and through him they had experienced sensations that they had rarely encountered in their lives until that moment. That is why the applause was lit with happiness.

# 8

## *The Great Home-coming*

Christoff has never left Bulgaria for any length of time, at least in his thoughts, so he does not return home like an exile, wanderer, refugee, repentant criminal or triumphant conqueror. He has kept the pain of absence to himself but his artistic triumphs have always been linked to Bulgaria. Those who believed in the middle of the 1970s that he had forgotten his native land had no conception of his artistic life. They cannot be aware of his innermost feelings, his longing to breathe the air of his native land and to wander around Mount Vitosha, to look at his reflection in the waters of Lake Rila, to laugh with his childhood friends or to withdraw to the silence of his lonely family home.

When in 1976 ancient liturgical chants were recorded in the Alexander Nevsky cathedral in Sofia, the notes accompanying the album described this recording as 'The Great Home-coming'. Perhaps these words were not precise, but it was generally recognized that this was a major event in the cultural life of the country: the recordings were a stage in the summing up of his accumulated experience and of his exploration of the ancient spiritual heritage of his homeland, and from that point of view it certainly represented a great return to his roots.

I can recall a gloomy evening at the villa of a lawyer, some time in July 1977. This villa was situated in Los Barcatello, perhaps the most beautiful corner of Monte Argentario. When I saw it for the first time from the hills above, I was convinced that it had been used in Italian films. The dusk had blocked out the horizon between the sea and the sky, and it was as if the same thing had happened to our thoughts. Christoff, who was spending the summer in a neighbouring villa, came up to us at the very moment when the contours had disappeared. He said: 'There are so many things that make me tired. I think that if I go into the sea I shan't ever come out again. Life is full of so many banal and stupid difficulties. On one side there are departments, on the other institutions and on the third offices....'

'But surely there are compensations. You have the applause of the public. You have your experiences!' Our host was trying to introduce some light into the gloom of our conversation, but he was unsuccessful.

'Yes! But how can we look at things from that point of view alone. Life has its hidden sides. I am truly exhausted.'

The conversation turned to Michelangeli, who was capable of cancelling a concert, even at the last minute, because he lived for the piano and not for concerts. Clearly nobody either expected or sought to find anything specific in this conversation and it would probably have continued in the same weary vein if Christoff had not noticed two of our host's books: *The History of the Byzantine Empire* by George

Ostrogorsky and *The History of the Middle Ages*. I had glanced through these books with our host during the day and they now lay on a table as if forgotten. Christoff bent over them in a rather bored manner and then began to leaf through them with growing excitement, and finally the sea and the sky parted as if frightened by his thoughts. At that moment no one expected lightning; but it appeared without reason, as in a surrealist painting....

'I have read some of this Ostrogorsky's works carefully. I underlined dozens of pages.... The worst thieves are those who steal a nation's history. They must be ignorant and bad people. How can they alter things which do not belong to them, but to us, to Bulgaria?'

On another occasion these words would have marked the beginning of an entertaining discussion with baroque twists and turns because the thieves, whether they were 'bad' or 'good', would have been long ago replaced by minstrels, suicides, knights or many other characters from literature.... But now developments could take only one direction. The lightning was transformed into sunlight and in Christoff's large and slightly reddened eyes one could see the reflection of warriors with helmets and shields who had come from afar, from the centuries of Bulgarian history. He looked at the miniatures which had been reproduced in the second book and commented in a loud voice. It was as if his hands were clutching a sword like that which had been the cause of his quarrel with Karajan and with which he was going to oppose all those who were trying to delay the advance of the Bulgarian warriors.

'Here under the feet of Vasil II, Slayer of the Bulgarians, these are Bulgarians. And the miniatures from the chronicles of Manassi in the Vatican? These people have reached the empire of Charles the Great. How can that ever be forgotten?

These theories of Ostrogorsky are ridiculous!'

At that moment Christoff did indeed resemble a general, and his sword cut through the misconceptions so that the sunlight of his truth could shine everywhere. No one present contradicted him but his blood pressure continued to rise. No other topic of conversation was thinkable. When he left he drove his Mercedes away at speed as if he were chasing someone. At that moment not one of us asked himself how all this had come about; but we were certain that it had not been 'created' for us.

I think that it was after these incidents that I began to have a better understanding of his patriotism. It was not a vague nostalgia or words spoken for effect, but something quite different. One might say it arose from a range of experiences, from the revolt of a true conscience to suppressed tears or to an outburst of joy at a revelation which had given a fresh meaning to his existence. Even when his words sounded like a declaration they were in fact a prayer.

On 2 July 1976 a small ceremony was held in the Bulgarian embassy in Rome to mark the award of the title of People's Artist to Christoff. He accepted the invitation without much thought but asked that only ten or so of his Italian friends should be invited. Everyone understood that he was not concerned about the ceremony itself but about the opportunities it offered for him to display his attitude to the award. There was something respectful in this idea since it allowed the guests to take part in the ceremony rather than merely be present at it. As the temporary chargé d'affaires at the embassy I had to say a few words of welcome and I recall that I felt a little awkward, since despite all my efforts they sounded rather official and therefore banal. There is nothing worse than discovering that you are not in control of your own thoughts.

However, Christoff soon set the right tone. When he stood before his friends he pronounced some words which I still remember: 'Ladies and gentlemen, I am happy that you are present at this intimate ceremony, which I consider to be a celebration. I am happy to see among you two people from this country who are dear to my heart: Professor Beniamino Guidetti, an exceptional scientist and surgeon, who with his deep knowledge and rare humanity saved my life ten years ago, and His Excellency Gabriele Pescatore, a dear friend at all times of my life, who at that time was able to be close to me, and who was also able to console my wife in her despair. To these feelings add my profound gratitude to Italy, which received me with love and gave me the opportunity to assimilate its ancient and rare culture, which stimulated my development as an artist and a man and opened the doors of the world's greatest musical institutions for me.'

Of his feeling for Bulgaria he said: 'I am very grateful to the Bulgarian state for the high honour that it has bestowed on me and for the touching feelings that lie behind it. My constant studies and my long international career have been and will always be on behalf of humanity, my Slavonic race and my native Bulgaria, towards whom I feel the devotion of a son and pride at her increased prestige.'

These words, spoken before his closest friends, were not a declaration but a confession. He, a man who had received ovations in so many countries of the world, was now, in these magnificent surroundings, as it were kneeling simply in order to kiss the finger which had touched him. On other occasions when I saw him bending over old travel notes, maps and engravings from his personal collection I once again connected him with the search for personal happiness on that road which connects him with his homeland.

On 12 October 1976 Christoff began the recording of

Bulgarian and Russian church music in the Alexander Nievsky cathedral in Sofia. In the course of about a week 'Evening Sacrifice' (music by Chesnokov), 'We Hymn Thee' (Zinoviev), 'Blessed is the Man' (Kochetov), 'Praise the name of the Lord' (D. Christoff), 'The Judicious Villain' (P. Dinev), 'The Great Glorification' (Nikolaev-Strumsky), 'Blessed Man' (Lyubimov) and 'Nunc Dimittis' (D. Christoff) were recorded.

The melodies he sang, expressing a consistent search for reconciliation and hope, had a humanity that warmed the spirits. The work on these recordings did not go as smoothly as he would have liked, but from the first Christoff eliminated any idea that a solo voice is inappropriate in this context. His beautiful bass, driven by some mystical strength, led powerfully with a broad vocal line. He calmed the senses with his rounded phrasing just as they were calmed by the closed lines of the old iconographic designs. Later he again took the listener in unexpected directions through his unusual psychological approach to the climaxes.

Some of the songs had been 'authorized' by the composers (Dobri Christoff, Petar Dinev, Nikolaev-Strumsky, Kochetov and Zinoviev). Others bore traces of alterations made during the recording itself. All these new interpretations, stylizations and amendments, however, did not change the fundamental character of the powerful moral-emotional and artistic inspiration, coming from a distant past, which at the present time cannot be 'modernized' without being reduced to absurdity. Just like the evolution of other art forms, the sacred music of Bulgaria of the Middle Ages developed under influence of specific stimuli, and the mass of the people frequently took a close and intimate interest in it, seeing it as the direct result of their collective and individual aesthetic experience.

Christoff interpreted these developments with great perception – as an aspiration for spiritual purity and elevated thinking, inspired by dramatic social conflicts and by the discoveries of enlightened reason. He thought it would be logical and symbolic to have as finale the life-affirming 'Many Years'. The optimism of this chant expressed a belief in the qualities of our people and in the triumph of the powerful human spirit far beyond the bounds of the future. As a kind of fusion with this future he entrusted the very end to the echo of the bells of the Alexander Nevsky cathedral.

So in the cathedral, to which no one had been officially invited and in which the 'audience' consisted of the centuries of the history of the great Bulgarian culture, Christoff sang for all those who had been captivated by his magnificent artistic gifts. Each day hundreds of people gathered outside the cathedral, and their interest was maintained not so much by reports on television and radio and in the press as by an admiration for his art and by a feeling of satisfaction that the constellation of Bulgarian talents had been enriched by his gifts. The recordings were an event in the cultural life of the country and many people saw in them a connection between the most brilliant creative achievements of our time and the inexhaustible resources of the ancient Bulgarian heritage.

When the recording equipment had been removed from the cathedral, there remained questions of organization, production and publicity. For Christoff, however, this was a continuation of the creative process. I recall how closely he was involved in the production of the notes accompanying the records and the captions for the sleeves. For many of those who bought the records this information may be of little interest. For Christoff, however, they could neither be avoided nor undervalued; he had always treated even the minor details of his work immensely seriously. Might it be thought that this was just another more-or-less successful recording in his remarkable career? His own reply made it clear that it was not! He wrote in the notes accompanying the record: 'The effort which I always apply to all of my artistic endeavours is a fruit of the impulse that drives me towards fulfilment of my aspirations – to succeed in my art and in this way to raise the spiritual and cultural level of my native Bulgaria, and to contribute, even a little, to the achievement of the eternal, world-wide desire: Peace on earth, goodwill towards men.'

The success of the first recording inspired fresh ideas, and in September 1979 Balkanton had at its disposal another record by Christoff: the *Domestic Liturgy* by Alexander Grechaninov. Discussions about this recording began, I believe, in spring 1977, and at first some misunderstandings arose. In July 1977, scores No. 1 and No. 2 of the work arrived in Rome along with some compositions by Dobri Christoff and Tchaikovsky. Fortunately the misunderstandings were quickly resolved and by the end of September 1978 the first part of the liturgy had been recorded. In addition to a Bulgarian choir, a small string section from the Bulgarian Radio Symphony Orchestra had been engaged.

It was the pioneering character of the recording of the *Domestic Liturgy* that transformed it into a significant event. The liturgy itself cannot be considered to be one of Grechaninov's most popular works. It has seldom been performed, and its emergence from the ranks of forgotten works is one of the more curious events of our musical life. Perhaps the disputes which had long raged over the 'orthodox' line of Eastern Orthodox Slavonic church music and the realization that its instrumental accompaniment was in conflict with its centuries-old tradition had not yet been forgotten.

But Christoff had carried with him the short, spiritually intimate songs by Grechaninov, along with some by Rachmaninov, ever since the time when he could be described as a 'travelling singer', overcoming great difficulties on his path to world fame. Later, in the mid-1960s, when he was making his first recordings of Russian church music in Paris, he once again turned his attention to them. As it happened he recorded only the *Domestic Liturgy* (known as 'A Special Litany'), but his interest had been transformed into a quest, the fulfilment of which he approached with the feeling of a discoverer.

Alexander Grechaninov was born in Moscow in 1864 and died in New York in 1956. He studied at the St Petersburg Conservatoire under Rimsky-Korsakov and later lived and worked in Moscow. He was a teacher at a music-school run by the Gnesin sisters as well as conductor of a children's choir in the music-school run by T.L. Berkman. During these years he wrote string works for children, operas and songs for choirs, and music for productions by the Moscow Art Theatre. In all these compositions one can find echoes of ancient Russian music. In the decades that followed, his compositions included six operas, cantatas, vocal-symphonic works, liturgies, sonatas, pieces for the piano and over 200 solo songs, romances and poems. Grechaninov lived in Paris from 1922 to 1939 and thereafter in the United States.

Christoff approached Grechaninov's work in his own particular way. When the question of Grechaninov's significance was raised, he pointed out that he saw in him 'a personal, typical style, especially in his sacred and secular vocal compositions'. Christoff rejected the views of 'certain ill-read musicologists' that Grechaninov had imitated the music of contemporaries such as Tchaikovsky, Debussy and others. He characterized the *Liturgia Demestvennaya*

(Domestic Liturgy) as a 'marvellous example of daring and success in interpreting ancient spiritual texts for our Orthodox liturgy'. In his view, Grechaninov introduced the orchestra into the liturgy in order to underline the nuances of its verbal content and to enrich with its own special harmonies the mystical mood necessary for spiritual discovery in a 'divine confession'. Deliberately using a reduced orchestra, Christoff maintained that Grechaninov 'relies on the artistic and spiritual power of his talent to add something extra to the spirituality of the Eastern Orthodox liturgy, and not to transform it into a symphonic composition on the principles of the West European masters of the Catholic Mass.' If we recall that this composition, which broke the traditions of Orthodox worship, was not allowed into the church and that the *Domestic Liturgy*, completed in 1917, was performed only in fragments (in the concert hall) in the West (as 'A Special Litany', it was performed by Chaliapin), we can understand the true significance of Christoff's achievement.

The composer entitled this liturgy 'Domestic' as an indication that it could be 'employed according to the requirements of every national Orthodox-Slavonic church independent of its Saints, Heads of State, military and state clergy'. Christoff grasped its moral and historic dimensions precisely because the performance of the liturgy made it specific and historically relevant.

The *Domestic Liturgy* was recorded in Sofia in the Alexander Nevsky cathedral. Christoff stood between two portraits that clearly had particular significance for him: Prince Boris and the great educators of the Slavs, Cyril and Methodius. For those who were controlling the recording equipment or who were directing things this fact scarcely had any value, but for the spirit of the songs which were being performed it had a certain symbolic meaning. Christoff's artistic presence, once happily described as 'massive', had as it were become stabilized under the influence of these images and he had made them 'advisers' in the attempt to 'preserve the Bulgarian people'. He sang facing the choir, but his gaze was steadily fixed upwards towards the West wall on which could be seen a representation of the Last Judgement. His voice rose towards it or descended from it. In this magnificent composition he did not appear to be the defendant nor yet the judge. He revealed the great responsibility with which he approached the task he had begun, and his obligations as an artist, as a Bulgarian and as a man.

Postscript

*In recent years Christoff has been living quietly in retirement in Rome, with Franca, as ever, beside him as helpmate. He is always willing to give advice to young singers, reminisce about the past, or simply enjoy a visitor's company. The importance of his achievement can now be realized in view of the absence of any true successor: what bass today encompasses his repetory or has the patience and knowledge to undertake the song repertoire performed by Christoff? He is truly one of the great singers and artists of the century.*

A.B.

# A Critical Discography

## by Alan Blyth

Records convincingly confirm Christoff's place as one of the most accomplished and imposing singers of the century, one who towers above almost all his successors and one who is on a par with the best of his predecessors. In Russian opera he inevitably recalls Chaliapin, much of whose repertory was similar to Christoff's; but Christoff was both the more sensitive musician and possibly (although I know this is controversial) the better technician. In Italian roles, his legato and his feeling for the language – Italy is, after all, his adopted home – place him in the true succession to Pinza and Pasero. But it is perhaps in Russian song that Christoff made his most significant contribution. No other singer before or since has taken the trouble to learn and project so comprehensibly all Mussorgsky's songs or to investigate so thoroughly the output of other Russian composers in this field – and then to have the wherewithal to do them justice.

Lord Harewood in his Foreword has characterized the astonishing impression that Christoff made on stage in a variety of roles, having been fortunate enough to catch Christoff in his absolute prime early in his career. It is the greatest good luck that some of the roles in live performances that he mentions have been preserved for posterity, albeit on minor labels. The earliest of these is his account of the bass part in the 1949 Salzburg Festival production of the Verdi *Requiem* under Karajan, where Christoff's imposing voice and very individual accents are already fully formed. Next comes his Procida in *I vespri Siciliani* recorded at the Maggio Musicale in 1951. Here, as well as anywhere, we can hear and estimate the strength of Christoff's presence on stage. With plenty of theatrical ambience, one can imagine the voice and presence mesmerizing the audience, and in the singing itself the familiar care for the character of a phrase and the timbre of a word can be truly felt. So it is again with his Oroveso (which he didn't record commercially) in the 1953 *Norma* at Trieste.

More important still is the assumption of Philip II at Covent Garden in the famous Visconti staging of *Don Carlos* in 1958: while the commercial sets may find the vocalization more equalized, for sheer impact of personality and opera-house tension – under Giulini's baton – the 1958 reading is essential listening, not quite matched by the 1960 Salzburg account. Two other important interpretations add further to the picture of Christoff as a Verdi singer: his properly earthy, pagan Attila and his Silva in *Ernani*, under that incomparable Verdian Dimitri Mitropoulos, from the Maggio in 1957 in which he catches the anger and sorrow of the old aristocrat. Both display Christoff's sovereign command of Verdian line and his thoroughly individual accents. The studio broadcast of *Parsifal* (in Italian) in 1950 is invaluable as a memento of another extraordinary portrayal, Christoff's fatherly Gurnemanz; not wholly idiomatic, perhaps, but stamped with the bass's customary authority. He sings with particular beauty in Act 3.

Although these glimpses of *opéra verité* are very precious, Christoff was such an accomplished performer in the studio, where he seemed to forget himself and think only of the character or song he was interpreting, that his many discs for EMI aptly enshrine his vocal and interpretative abilities. Virtually everything that he did, much of it under the watchful eye and ear of Walter Legge, the perceptive and enlightened EMI producer, is alive, spontaneous, never in the least studio-bound. And that was true from the outset of his career with HMV, as EMI then was. Until near the end of his recording life Christoff was, with the exception of his second recording of *Don Carlos*, faithful to the company that helped him establish his career in the closing years of the 78rpm era. All his discs made at this time, between 1949 and 1952, including some previously unpublished items, appeared in the 1979 LP box RLS735, issued to mark his 30 years with the company.

This is as rewarding a conspectus of his work as any. It begins with a gallery of his best-loved roles in Russian opera. The very first band, Susanin's monologue, announces Christoff's extraordinary fidelity to the verities of fine singing – the essential alliance between words and line, the control of dynamics, the innate feeling for character. Christoff used to tell me that he wanted to show London his skills in Glinka's opera; sadly that was not to be. Gremin's aria, though taken a shade too fast because of the exigencies of 78rpm, is lovingly phrased, one of Tchaikovsky's most glorious melodies rolled out gratefully before us. Christoff loved to sing both the libidinous Galitsky and the generous-hearted Konchak in *Prince Igor* (he later did so on a complete set – see Discography), and here in their respective solos he unerringly contrasts the bold, outrageous personality of the one, the joviality of the other. Then his version of The Song of the Viking Guest from *Sadko* rivals that by Chaliapin in its ebullient attack, while the aria from Rimsky's *Kitezh* shows once more Christoff's gifts for interior feeling.

The four bands on side 2 date from Christoff's earliest sessions in London. His singing of solos from all three bass roles – Boris, Pimen and Varlaam – in *Boris Godunov* predates Christoff's assumption of these parts in the 1952 recording of the whole opera. The singing of Boris's three main solos already discloses his command of the role in terms of authoritative declamation, intensity of utterance and well-schooled phrasing. They were made months before his stage début in the role at Covent Garden in November 1949; it is extraordinary that he should have such a deep understanding of its needs before playing it in the opera house. Whatever one may think of the advisability of his also singing Pimen and Varlaam in a complete set, the solos heard here individually show Christoff able to differentiate between the troubled Tsar, the venerable monk and the roistering peasant. Next on the LP set comes a properly solemn account of Dosifey's aria from Act 4 of Mussorgsky's *Khovanshchina*.

In spite of his familiarity with and understanding of the Russian repertory, Christoff from the beginning of his career determined to give equal time and attention to other repertory. So we hear him on the third side of the LP box as a baleful, black-browed Agamemnon in Gluck's *Iphigénie in Aulide*, where the voice is powerful, almost threatening.

Then in complete contrast he lightens and alters his tone for Mozart's disreputable Leporello, telling, with delight and delicate nuance, the tale of Don Giovanni's conquests. But most important here are the Verdi items. Silva's solo 'Infelice' from *Ernani* has seldom been sung with such fervour. Christoff adds the rousing cabaletta, at that time something of a rarity in performance of this opera. Both verses are dispatched with great verve. Procida's greeting to his beloved Sicily in 'O tu Palermo' from *Vespri* matches the version on the live recording already mentioned; the cries 'A vittoria, all'onor' are full of the conviction of the fanatical nationalist.

Then comes his first account of Philip II's moving monologue from *Don Carlos*. Conducted by Karajan, no less, this demonstrates at once Christoff's command of vocal colour. He begins it with a tone that is private, soft, tender, altering to the more expansive and sorrowful at 'amor per me non ha'. As a whole the performance shows the sad king as solitary and withdrawn, his world become grey and lonely. Later the reading, in his two complete sets of the opera, became more refined and even deeper, eliminating the occasional touches of melodrama indulged in here by the younger artist.

A complete contrast comes with the next two bands, where Christoff adopts a sardonic, biting tone for the title role in Boito's *Mefistofele*. These exhibit his gift for pointed characterization. John Steane graphically described Christoff's performance of these solos in his book *The Grand Tradition*: 'marvellously sonorous, ringing and effortlessly sustained on the high F sharp, agile in its devilry without sacrificing the fine, resonant tone'.

From here onwards RLS735 encompasses Christoff's appreciable achievement in song already evident in his early years, starting with a previously unissued account of Beethoven's *In questa tomba oscura* that has all the gravity and presence the song requires. Most of the discs of Russian song were not issued at the time they were made; which, considering their calibre, is incomprehensible. For each of the Mussorgsky songs, Christoff finds precisely the right style and mood. The sharp-eyed, sardonic humour of *The Seminarist*, the sombre thoughts of *The Grave*, the gloom of *The wind howls*, the fantastic humour of *The Song of the Flea* all become vivid in Christoff's readings. The three songs by Borodin, all welcome on disc, are sung with the lyrical impulse they call for, while the histrionic force of Rimsky's *The Prophet* is fully realized. Later Christoff would further refine his style, but already here he is master of the genre.

With the advent of LP, the possibilities for Christoff to display his vocal and interpretative skills on disc were, of course, greatly enhanced. Quite rightly his first complete set on LP (1952) was of *Boris Godunov*, a performance to which I have already referred. It is generally considered the better of his two interpretations, not least because of the authoritative and inspiriting direction of Issay Dobrowen, who died all too young the following year. His reading is taut and authentically Russian in timbre. Christoff, obviously influenced by the vast shade of Chaliapin, who had dominated the role of the Tsar in the previous generation, is yet his own man in creating a vivid portrait of the guilt-ridden, tormented Boris. As I have already reported, Christoff also undertook the parts of Pimen and Varlaam in this (and the later, 1962, account under Cluytens). It is a questionable procedure only partially justified by Christoff's extraordinary skill in varying his tone to describe the very different personalities of the three characters. Although there may be greater refinements in Christoff's 1963 Boris,

Cluytens is not such an idiomatic conductor and the supporting cast is markedly inferior. Where it scores is in giving the Rimsky version complete while Dobrowen makes the cuts standard in the theatre at the time.

Christoff's first recording of *Faust* soon followed. As Méphistophélès here and in the stereo remake Christoff exudes a tremendous presence as the devil incarnate. Whatever we may feel about his idiosyncratic French, he announced from his very first phrase, 'me voici', the arrival of a satanic and other-worldly force. To quote Steane (*op cit*) again: 'One sees his smile, shares his fun, knows exactly when he has arrived at the Kermesse – he never needs to announce "me voici" again'.

In 1954 Christoff's first recording of *Don Carlos* appeared. Philip II was the role, Boris apart, in which he was most frequently encountered at Covent Garden and elsewhere. In it he commanded the stage by virtue of his superb acting. The doleful presence hardly masked the zeal of the king in imposing his authority on his unhappy wife, son and antagonist (Rodrigo). Only the Grand Inquisitor, in their great fourth-act colloquy, could impose a greater authority, the Church's as against the State's. Somehow Christoff managed to transfer to disc the variety and acumen of his reading. Lord Harewood in *Opera on Record* (Hutchinson, 1979) put it thus: 'Christoff ... has a rare intensity and focus, and re-hearing this set convinces me that his full, fervent phrasing and ability to use the text bring him nearer than anyone else in their generation to rivalling the operatic *completeness* of Maria Callas – two foreigners on the Italian scene! His soft singing is perhaps the most expressive weapon in his vocal armoury, but in King Philip restraint and understatement count for much.' His portrayal is perhaps at its most potent in his verbal duel with Tito Gobbi's Rodrigo.

Although it is out of chronology it may be as well to deal
here with the 1961 remake (for Deutsche Grammophon) on
which Christoff repeats his Philip II, where he shows
perhaps an even greater range of vocal address.

His next appearance in a complete opera was, fortuitous-
ly, in Verdi's next opera *Aïda*, in which Christoff plays the
high priest Ramphis. This is part of a set, with Zinka Milanov
as Aïda, Jussi Björling as Radames and Leonard Warren as
Amonasro, that remains one of the most satisfying
realizations of the opera on record. Above all Ramphis calls
for authority and declamatory force: these Christoff
provides in abundance in an account of the role that has
seldom been equalled except by the likes of Pinza and
Pasero. That set was made in Rome in July 1955. Two
months later Christoff was in the studios again in the Italian
capital to record a recital of Italian arias and Boito's
*Mefistofele*. The recital gives us glimpses of Christoff in roles
that he did not record, at any rate 'officially'. He sang
Zaccaria in Verdi's *Nabucco* at Chicago in 1963 in one of his
all-too-rare American appearances. His versions of Zaccaria's two major solos – the first urging the Israelites to curb
their tears, the second prophesying Judah's triumph over
Babylon – have seldom if ever been intoned with such power
and authority as by Christoff in this recital, nor has Padre
Guardiano's solo from Act 2 of Verdi's *La forza del destino*
been delivered with such pointed diction, such imposing
tone as here, nor Oroveso's solo from Bellini's *Norma* had
such a noble profile, nor Count Rodolfo's cavatina from the
same composer's *La Sonnambula* been given with such
serene stillness, though Steane here misses an Italian bass's
'richly honeyed sound'. The final item on the recital is
Fiesco's solo from the Prologue to Verdi's *Simon Boccanegra*.
Harewood (*op cit*) declares it 'an improvement on that in the

complete recording', which was in fact to follow two years later.

Boito's idea of Mephistopheles is grist to Christoff's mill. As on those 78rpm excerpts, Christoff is magnificent, catching the quirkiness of the character as delineated by the composer. This set has never had a very general distribution: it should now reappear on CD. Happily the famous *Simone Boccanegra*, again made in Rome, has appeared on CD, excellently transferred. Here Christoff's pungent, crisply articulated singing is ideally suited to the proud, implacable patrician. His reading shades into deeply felt remorse in the final, conciliatory meeting with Boccanegra (splendidly interpreted by Gobbi). Fiesco was one of Christoff's triumphs in the opera house: here it is admirably caught for posterity.

Later in 1957, Christoff returned to his beloved Russian for his next operatic offering – Glinka's *A Life for the Tsar*, also known as *Ivan Susanin*. Two years later he was to take the role of Susanin with great success on stage at La Scala. Once more Christoff creates a credible character, the sympathetic peasant hero, in terms of sound alone. His final complete recording of opera for EMI was *Prince Igor* in 1966, where his famous doubling, already referred to, of the roles of Prince Galitsky and Khan Konchak is presented in more rounded terms than on the 78rpm records. In 1972 Christoff added to his laurels, and further proved his versatility, with his performance as Saul in Unicorn's trail-blazing set of Nielsen's *Saul and David*, where the bass's voice seems in admirable condition. His final opera recording, a recital, was made in Sofia in 1979 for Balkanton/Forlane. At 65, Christoff's voice had lost some power but little of its inherent quality – and, of course, all the old authority and intelligence are present. This LP fills in some gaps in discs of his repertory, most importantly in respect of Seneca's long and moving death scene from Monteverdi's *L'Incoronazione di Poppea*, sung with deep eloquence, Pizarro's outburst from *Fidelio* (a biting interpretation that reminds us of one of the singer's earliest roles), and Banquo's disturbed aria from Verdi's *Macbeth*.

Christoff's other great contribution to recording history, perhaps even more vital than his opera assumptions, is his corpus of discs of Russian song, simply because – to date – this is a unique achievement. To discuss the performance of each song would be both self-defeating and in any case beyond the scope of this survey. All I shall do is to give some detailed coverage of the most important of these issues, the complete set of Mussorgsky songs, particularly as this is available on CD, and then indicate the extent of the remainder of Christoff's recordings in this field.

The Mussorgsky songs were recorded in Paris between 1955 and 1957, with Alexandre Labinsky at the piano. Listening through the set without a break gives one some idea of the amazing variety of Mussorgsky's writing, and leaves one even more astonished at Christoff's vocal virtuosity.

Mussorgsky's range of characterization is veritably Dostoyevskian. Even on the first disc, in the earlier and less remarkable songs, the composer offers a range of characters and emotions until then unknown in Russian song. Appearing before us, among many others, are the warlike *King Saul*, the sad figure of Wilhelm Meister in the *Song of the Old Man* ('An die Türen' in the original German), the desolate landscape of *The wind howls* (see also the 78 version above), the folk-hero Calistratus. The variety of styles is equally revelatory, from the recitative of *Cast-off Woman* to the gentle lyricism of *Night*. In this last song,

Christoff produces that magical *mezza voce*, which was always such a feature of his singing, to suggest the intimacy of the loved one portrayed within – but by then, the eleventh song, he has already shown an amazing palette of sound-colours, everything from the bitterly ferocious to the gentlest whisper.

With the second CD we come to many of the well-known pieces. Few have been better interpreted than here. In *Gopak*, Christoff has a high old time, relishing every word. In *Savishna*, a peculiarly vivid song, he gives a subtle portrayal of the idiot. He encompasses the bitter satire of *The Classicist* and, as on the 78 version, the humour of *The Seminarist*, where the Latin recitation is gleefully declaimed. *Puppet Show*, a somewhat weak song, is rescued here by Christoff's identity with its ironic twists. Then he changes style again to produce a hypnotically sweet timbre for *Evening Song*, a tender lyric built on just five notes.

The centrepiece of this disc is the *Nursery* cycle, where Christoff amazingly reduces and adapts his big voice for a convincing impersonation of a small boy, and he finds yet another timbre for the nurse and the mother. Indeed his characterization is so pointed that it seems as if he is in the room with you making the appropriate grimaces. This is a *tour-de-force*. On the third CD are to be found more predictably rewarding accounts of the *Sunless* and *Songs and Dances of Death* cycles. We hear all the bleak gloom of the first, the histrionic force of the second, again remarkable for the range of tone. The merit of his singing excuses the corrupt orchestration. As Steane comments (*op cit*), for Death Christoff 'has a darkness and depth of voice and a grim fund of merriment'. Of the final song of the *Sunless* cycle, entitled 'On the River', Steane writes: 'Each phrase has its own colour. The most majestic of voices becomes the most gentle: the superb work of a golden-age singer.'

After these cycles Mussorgsky's inspiration seemed to falter, though *On the Dnieper*, a melodious song of surpassing beauty, and the ever popular *Song of the Flea*, at the end of this absorbing set, are splendid pieces excellently interpreted by Christoff. The original LP set printed Christoff's knowledgeable notes on the songs; sadly, these are excluded from the CD reissue.

The singer's service to Mussorgsky would be achievement enough for a lesser singer, but Christoff was tireless in his efforts to record, in both senses, the work of Russian composers in the field of song and made discs of songs by Glinka, Tchaikovsky, Borodin, Rachmaninov, Cui, Balakirev, Grechaninov, and Rimsky-Korsakov. He brings to each composer a sympathy and understanding equal and similar to that he gave to Mussorgsky as has been noted in the main text. In each case the voice is in fine fettle, and each poem has been studied carefully for its interior meaning, while matching the demands of its setting. These neglected performances demand reissue on CD: they are unlikely to be matched, let alone surpassed, in the foreseeable future. In parenthesis, as it were, one should note Christoff's fervent, moving account of the baritone (!) solos in an Italian performance of Brahms's *Requiem* in 1952, conducted by Bruno Walter.

As a pendant to this recording achievement in the major repertory, one should not overlook Christoff's contribution to the music of his country of birth. This is another area in which a successor will be hard to find.

# Discography

# by Malcolm Walker

1949 May 19–20. EMI Studio No 1, 3 Abbey Road, London NW8
Philharmonia Orchestra/Issay Dobrowen
   Mussorgsky: *Boris Godunov*: Boris's Monologue
      78: HMV DB6948; RCA set DM1436
      45: RCA EHA11
      LP: HMV RLS735; Electrola WBLP1008, Electrola 1C 147
      03336/7M; VdP QBLP5002
      MC: HMV TC-RLS735
   Mussorgsky: *Boris Godunov*: Farewell
      78: HMV DB6935; RCA set DM1436
      45: HMV 7R114; Electrola 7RW135
      LP: HMV BLP1003, RLS735; Electrola WBLP1008. E70018. 1C
      147 03336/7M; VdP QBLP5002
      MC: HMV TC-RLS735
   Mussorgsky: *Boris Godunov*: Death of Boris
      78: HMV DB21097
      45: PM 7RF105, 7RF166
      LP: HMV BLP1003, RLS735; Electrola WBLP1003, E70018, 1C
      147 03336/7M; VdP QBLP5002
      MC: HMV TC-RLS735

Boito: *Mefistofele*: Ave Signor!
  78: HMV DB21047
  45: PM 7RF263
  LP: HMV RLS735; Electrola 1C 147 03336/7M; PM FALP322
  MC: HMV TC-RLS735

1949 August 14. Salzburg Festival: Festspielhaus [public performance]
  Hilde Zadek (*sop*); Margarete Klose (*mez*); Helge Roswaenge (*ten*); Vienna State Opera Chorus; Vienna Philharmonic Orchestra/Herbert von Karajan
  Verdi: Requiem Mass
    LP: Rococo RR391; Cetra LO524
    CD: Rodolphe RP12403/4

1949 November 28. Kingsway Hall, Kingsway, London WC2
  Philharmonia Orchestra/Herbert von Karajan
    Gounod: *Faust*: Vous qui faîtes l'endormie unpublished [2EA14333-1]
    Mussorgsky: *Boris Godunov*: In the town of Kazan (Varlaam's Song)
      78: HMV DB21097; RCA set DM1436
      45: RCA EHA111; PM 7RF166
      LP: HMV BLP1003, RLS735; Electrola WBLP1005; VdP QBLP5002.
      MC: HMV TC-RLS735
    Verdi: *Don Carlos*: Ella giammai m'amò ... Dormiro sol
      78: HMV DB21007
      45: PM 7RF262
      LP: HMV RLS735; Electrola 1C 147 03336/7M; PM FALP322
      MC: HMV TC-RLS735

1949 December 3. EMI Studio No 1
  Philharmonia Orchestra/Nicolai Malko
    Boito: *Mefistofele*: Son lo spirito che nega
      78: HMV DB21047
      45: PM 7RF263
      LP: HMV RLS735; PM FALP322; Electrola 1C 147 03336/7M
      MC: HMV TC-RLS735
    Mussorgsky: *Boris Godunov*: Pimen's Monologue
      78: HMV DA1938
      45: PM 7RF213

LP: HMV RLS735

MC: HMV TC-RLS735

1949 December 4. EMI Studio No 3, 3 Abbey Road, London NW8
Gerald Moore (pf)

Mussorgsky: *Songs and Dances of Death*: No 1, Trepak unpublished
[2EA14352-1, -2]

Mussorgsky: *Songs and Dances of Death* No 4, Field-Marshal Death
unpublished [2EA14353-1, -2; 2EA14354-1]

1950 May 4. EMI Studio No 1
Philharmonia Orchestra/Issay Dobrowen

Rimsky-Korsakov: *Khovanshchina*: Dosifey's Aria

78: HMV DB21207

45: HMV 7ER5007, 7R136; VdP 7ERQ132; PM 7RF165

LP: HMV RLS735; RCA LHMV1033; PM FALP322; Electrola
1C 147 03336/7M

MC: HMV TC-RLS735

Rimsky-Korsakov: *Sadko*: Song of the Viking Guest

78: HMV DB21117

45: HMV 7R150

LP: PM FALP322; HMV RLS735; Electrola 1C 147 147 03336/
7M

MC: HMV TC-RLS735

1950 May 5
Philharmonia Orchestra/Issay Dobrowen

Borodin: *Prince Igor*: How goes it, Prince? (Konchak's aria)

78: HMV DB21626

45: HMV 7ER5007, 7R125; PM 7ERQ132, 7RF164; Electrola
7RW111

LP: HMV BLP1003, RLS735; VdP QBLP5002; Electrola 1C 147
03336/7M

MC: HMV TC-RLS735

1950 May 8
Philharmonia Orchestra/Issay Dobrowen

Borodin: *Prince Igor*: I hate a dreary life (Prince Galitsky's aria)

78: HMV DB21117

45: HMV 7ER5007, 7R150; PM 7ERQ107, 7RQ3030; PM
7RF163; Electrola 7RW134

LP: HMV BLP1003, RLS735; Electrola WBLP1003, E70018, 1C

147 03336/7M; VdP QBLP5002
MC: HMV TC-RLS735

1950 May 16. EMI Studio No 3
Gerald Moore (*pf*)
Borodin: *Queen of the Sea*
LP: HMV RLS735
MC: HMV TC-RLS735

1950 May 17. EMI Studio No 3
Gerald Moore (*pf*)
Borodin: 'Home to thy native land'
LP: HMV RLS735
MC: HMV TC-RLS735
Borodin: *The Sleeping Princess*
LP: HMV RLS735
MC: HMV TC-RLS735

1950 October 5. Kingsway Hall
Philharmonia Orchestra/Issay Dobrowen
Rimsky-Korsakov: *The Prophet*, Op 49/2
LP: HMV RLS735
MC: HMV TC-RLS735
Traditional: 'Song of the Volga boatmen'
78: HMV DB21305
45: HMV 7R143; PM 7RF214, ESBF17028
LP: HMV RLS735; Electrola 1C 147 03336/7M
MC: HMV TC-RLS735
Mussorgsky (orch Rimsky-Korsakov): *Song of the Flea*
78: HMV DB21305
45: HMV 7R143; PM 7RF214, ESBF17028
LP: HMV RLS735; Electrola 1C 147 03336/7M
MC: HMV TC-RLS735

1950 November 20–21. Broadcast studio performances. Rome
Africo Baldelli (*ten*) Parsifal; Maria Callas (*sop*) Kundry; Rolando
Panerai (*bar*) Amfortas; BC (*bass*) Gurnemanz; Dimitri Lopatto (*bass*)
Titurel; Giuseppe Modesti (*bass*) Klingsor; Rome RAI Chorus and
Orchestra/Vittorio Gui
Wagner: *Parsifal*
LP: Penzance FWR648; Foyer 1002; Estro Armonico EA55;
MWC101

CD: Melodram MEL36.041

1951 March 3. EMI Studio No 3

  Gerald Moore (*pf*)

    Mussorgsky: *The Grave* (Sadly rustled the leaves)

      78: HMV DB21383

      45: HMV 74161; RCA WHMV1033; PM 7RF261; VdP 7RQ3030

      LP: RCA LHMV1033; HMV RLS735

      MC: HMV TC-RLS735

      CD: EMI CHS7 63025-2

    Mussorgsky: *Softly the spirit flew up to Heaven*

      78: HMV DB21484

      45: RCA WHMV1033

      LP: RCA LHMV1033; RLS735

      MC: HMV TC-RLS735

    Mussorgsky: *Songs & Dances of Death* No. 4, Field-Marshal Death

      78: HMV DB21484

      LP: HMV RLS735; Electrola 1C 147 03336/7M

      MC: HMV TC-RLS735

    Traditional: 'Siberian Prisoner's Song'

      78: HMV DB21383

      45: RCA WHMV1033

      LP: RCA LHMV1033; HMV RLS735

      MC: HMV TC-RLS735

1951 March 6. Kingsway Hall

  Philharmonia Orchestra/Anatole Fistoulari

    Gluck: *Iphigénie en Aulide*: O Diane impitoyable [Ital]

      LP: HMV RLS735

      MC: HMV TC-RLS735

    Verdi: *Ernani*: Che mai veggio ... Infelice

      78: HMV DB21424

      45: PM 7RF264; VdP 7RQ264

      LP: PM FALP322; HMV RLS735; Electrola 1C 147 03336/7M

      MC: HMV TC-RLS735

1951 May 26. Live performance. Teatro Comunale. Florence

  Maria Callas (*sop*) Elena; Giorgio Kokolios-Bardi (*ten*) Arrigo: Enzo Mascherini (*bar*) Monforte; BC (Procida); Bruno Carmassi (*bass*) Bethune; Maggio Musicale Fiorentino Chorus and Orchestra/Erich Kleiber

Verdi: *I Vespri siciliani*
    LP: Penzance FWR645; MRF MRF46; Penzance 6; Estro Armonico EA018; Cetra LO-5; Turnabout THS65134/36
1952 March 17. EMI Studio No 1
  Philharmonia Orchestra/Wilhelm Schüchter
    Mozart: *Don Giovanni*: Madamina
      78: HMV DA2080
      LP: HMV RLS735; Electrola 1C 147 03336/7M
      MC: HMV TC-RLS735
1952 March 18. EMI Studio No 1
  Philharmonia Orchestra/Wilhelm Schüchter
    Verdi: *I Vespri siciliani*: O tu, Palermo
      LP: HMV RLS735
      MC: HMV TC-RLS735
1952 March 19. EMI Studio No 1
  Philharmonia Orchestra/Wilhelm Schüchter
    Tchaikovsky: *Eugene Onegin*: Everyone knows love on earth (Prince Gremin's aria)
      78: DB21626
      LP: HMV RLS735
      MC: HMV TC-RLS735
    Rimsky-Korsakov: *The Legend of the Invisible City of Kitezh*: O vain illusion
      78: HMV DB21626
      45: RCA WHMV1033
      LP: RCA LHMV1033; HMV RLS735; Electrola 1C 147 03336/7M
      MC: HMV TC-RLS735
1952 March 19
  Philharmonia Orchestra/Wilhelm Schüchter
    Glinka: *Life for the Tsar*: They guess the truth
      LP: HMV RLS735
      MC: HMV TC-RLS735
    Rimsky-Korsakov: *The Prophet*, Op 49/2 unpublished [2EA16405]
1952 March 28. EMI Studio No 3
  Gerald Moore (*pf*)
    Caldara: 'Come raggio di sol'
      78: HMV DB21592

LP: HMV RLS735; Electrola 1C 147 03336/7M
MC: HMV TC-RLS735
Mussorgsky (ed Karatvgin): *The wind howls*
  LP: HMV RLS735
  MC: HMV TC-RLS735
1952 March 29
  Gerald Moore (*pf*)
  Beethoven: *In questa tomba oscura*, Wo0133 unpublished
  [OEA164443]
  Lishkin: 'She mocked'
    78: HMV DB21592
    LP: HMV RLS735
    MC: HMV TC-RLS735
  Mussorgsky (arr Rimsky-Korsakov): *The Song of the Flea*
    LP: HMV RLS735
    MC: HMV TC-RLS735
1952 March 30
  Gerald Moore (*pf*)
  Beethoven: *In questa tomba oscura*, Wo0133
    LP: HMV RLS735
    MC: HMV TC-RLS735
  Koeneman: 'When the King went forth to war'
    LP: HMV RLS735
    MC: HMV TC-RLS735
  Mussorgsky: *The Seminarist*
    LP: HMV RLS735
    MC: HMV TC-RLS735
1952 April 16. Broadcast performance, Rome
  Rosanna Carteri (*sop*); BC; Rome RAI Chorus and Orchestra/Bruno
  Walter
    Brahms: *Ein deutsches Requiem* (sung in Italian)
    LP: Fonit-Cetra LAR7
1952 July 6–21. Théâtre des Champs-Elysées, Paris
  Eugenia Zareska (*mez*) Marina; Nicolai Gedda (*ten*) Dmitri; BC Boris,
  Pimen and Varlaam; Andrei Bielecki (*ten*) Shuisky; Kim Borg (*bass*)
  Rangoni, Shchelkalov; Vassili Pasternak (*bass*) The Simpleton;
  Choeurs Russes de Paris; French Radio National Orchestra/Issay
  Dobrowen

Mussorgsky: *Boris Godunov*
>  45: RCA WHMV6400
>  LP: HMV ALP1044/7; ALP1323 (excs), SLS5072; RCA LHMV6400, LHMV1052 (excs), LVT1021 (excs); Capitol GDR7164; Seraphim ID6101; PM FALP184/7, FALP30153 (excs); Electrola WALP1044/7; VdP 3C 153 14161/4M

1953 October 22–26. Salle Mutualité, Paris
Victoria de los Angeles (*sop*) Marguerite; Nicolai Gedda (*ten*) Faust; Jean Borthayre (*bar*) Valentin; BC Méphistophélès; Marthe Angelici (*sop*) Siébel; Solange Michel (*mez*) Marthe; Paris Opera Chorus and Orchestra/André Cluytens

>  Gounod: *Faust*
>  45: HMV 7ER5078 (excs)
>  LP: HMV ALP1162/5; RCA LM6403, LM1825 (excs); PM FALP261/4

1953 November. Live performance. Teatro Giuseppe Verdi, Trieste
Maria Callas (*sop*) Norma; Elena Nicolai (*mez*) Adalgisa: Franco Corelli (*ten*) Pollione; BC (Oroveso); Bruna Ronchini (*sop*) Clothilde; Raimondo Botteghelli (*ten*) Flavio; Chorus and Orchestra of Teatro Giuseppe Verdi, Trieste/Antonino Votto

>  Bellini: *Norma* – abridged
>  LP: Hist Rec Ent HRE283

1954 June 6. Live performance. Teatro Comunale, Florence
Magda Olivero (*sop*) Maria; Mariana Radev (*mez*) Lyubov; David Poleri (*ten*) Andrei; Ettore Bastianini (*bar*) Mazeppa; BC Kochubey; Fausto Flamini (*ten*) Iskra; Giorgio Algorta (*bass*) Orlik; Piero De Palma (*ten*) Cossack; Maggio Musicale Fiorentino Chorus and Orchestra/Jonel Perlea

>  Tchaikovsky: *Mazeppa* (sung in Italian)
>  LP: Cetra LO43

1954 September–October. Salle Mutualité
*Balalaika ensemble
>  'Russian Songs'
>  Grechaninov: *Litany*
>  Traditional: 'Song of the lumberjacks'; 'The Bandore'; 'Going down the Volga'; 'The Lonely Autumn Night'; Psalm 137: By the waters of Babylon; 'Prayer to St Simeon'; 'Lord, have mercy on our people'; 'The Song of the 12 Robbers' (Siberian song; arr Potorzhinsky);

'Shrove Tuesday'*; 'Down Peterskaya Street'*

    LP: HMV ALP1266; PM FALP351, FALP30045; Victor LM1945

1954 October 5–20. Opera House, Rome

    Antonietta Stella (*sop*) Elisabetta; Elena Nicolai (*mez*) Eboli; Mario Filippeschi (*ten*) Don Carlos; Tito Gobbi (*bar*) Rodrigo; BC Philip II; Giulio Neri (*bass*) Grand Inquisitor; Plinio Clabassi (*bass*) The Monk; Rome Opera Chorus and Orchestra/Gabriele Santini

    Verdi: *Don Carlos* (four-act version)

        LP: HMV ALP1289/92, ALP1700 (excs); RCA LM6124; PM FALP400/03; Seraphim IC6004

        1954 Broadcast performance, Turin

            Elisabeth Schwarzkopf, Luigia Vincenti (*sops*); Miriam Pirazzini (*mez*); Cesare Valietti (*ten*); BC; Turin RAI Chorus and Orchestra/Mario Rossi Mozart: *La betulia liberata*, K118/K47c

        CD: Nuova Era 2377

1955 March, April and June; 1956 April–May; 1957 March Salle Mutualité, Paris

    [a]Alexandre Labinsky (pf); [b]French Radio National Orchestra/Georges Tzipine

        Mussorgsky: 'But if I could meet thee again'[a]; 'Child's Song'[a]; The Classicist[a]; 'Darling Savishna'[a]; 'Dear one, why are thine eyes so cold?'[a]; 'Epitaph'[a]; 'Eremushka's lullaby'[a]; 'Evening song'[a]; 'The feast'[a]; 'Forgotten'[a]; 'From my tears'[a]; 'The garden by the Don'[a]; 'Gathering mushrooms'[a]; 'Gopak'[b]; 'Hebrew song'[a]; 'The he-goat: a worldly story'[a]; 'Hour of jollity'[a]; 'I have many palaces and gardens'[a]; 'Is spinning man's work?'[a]; 'It scatters and breaks'[a]; 'Kalistratushka'[a]; 'King Saul'[b]; 'Lullaby'[a]; 'The magpie'[a]; 'Mephistopheles' song of the flea'[b]; 'Night'[a]*; 'Not like thunder trouble struck'[a]; 'The nursery'[a]; 'Old man's song'[a]; 'On the Dnieper'[a]; 'The orphan'[a]; 'The outcast'[a]; 'The peepshow'[a]; 'A prayer'[a]; 'Pride'[a]; 'The ragamuffin'[a]; 'Sadly rustled the leaves'[a]; 'The seminarist'[a]; 'Softly the spirit flew up to heaven'[a]; 'Songs of death'[b]; 'The sphinx'[a]; *Sunless*[a]; 'Tell me why, o maiden'[a]; 'The vision'[a]; 'The wanderer'[a]; 'What are words of love to you?'[a]; 'Where art thou, little star?'[a]; 'The wild wind blows'[b]

        LP: PM FALP489/92; Angel DLX3575; HMV ALP1652/5; Electrola 1C 137 173164-3. *ASD2559

        CD: EMI CHS7 63025-2

1955 July 2, 4, 6, 8–9, 11–13, 15–18. Opera House, Rome

Zinka Milanov (*sop*) Aïda; Fedora Barbieri (*mez*) Amneris; Jussi Björling (*ten*) Radames; Leonard Warren (*bar*) Amonasro; BC Ramfis; Plinio Clabassi (*bass*) King of Egypt; Rome Opera Chorus and Orchestra/ Jonel Perlea

Verdi: *Aïda*

LP: HMV ALP1388/90; RCA LM6122; VL43533; LM6069 (excs); RB6585 (excs); VIC6119

MC: RCA 4AV-5380

CD: RCA GD86652; GD60201

1955 October 10–11 and 19–20. Opera House, Rome

Rome Opera Chorus and Orchestra/Vittorio Gui

Bellini: *Norma*: Ite sul colle, o Druidi[a]

Bellini: *La Sonnambula*: Il mulino … Vi ravviso[b]

Verdi: *La Forza del destino*: Il santo nome di Dio[c]

Verdi: *Nabucco*: O chi piange? … Del futuro[d]

Verdi: *Nabucco*: Sperate, o figli … D'Egitto la sui lidi[e]

Verdi: *Simon Boccanegra*: A te l'estremo addio … Il lacerato spirito[f]

LP: HMV ALP1585,[acde] SLS5090, [e]EX7 69741-1; Capitol G7125

MC: [acde]TC-SLS5090

1955 October 12–19. Opera House, Rome

BC Mefistofele; Giacinto Prandelli (*ten*) Faust; Orietta Moscucci (*sop*) Margherita; Rome Opera Chorus and Orchestra/Vittorio Gui

Boito: *Mefistofele*

LP: HMV ALP1369/70; RCA LM6040

1955 October 22 (recorded); December 10 (broadcast)

Rina Corsi (*mez*) Marina; Mirto Picchi (*ten*) Dmitri; BC Boris; Giuseppe Modesti (*bass*) Pimen; Dimitri Lopatto (*bass*) Varlaam; Angelo Mercuriali (*ten*) Shuisky, The Simpleton; Fernando Valentini (*bar*) Shchelkalov; Rome RAI Chorus and Orchestra/Artur Rodzinski

Mussorgsky: *Boris Godunov*

LP: HOPE 220

1956 Opera House, Rome (live performance)

Clara Petrella (*sop*) Iris; Giuseppe di Stefano (*ten*) Osaka; Saturno Meletti (*bar*) Kyoto; BC Il Cieco; Aida Hovnanian; Adelio Zagonara; Piero de Palma Rome Opera Chorus & Orch/Gianandrea Gavazzeni

Mascagni: *Iris*

LP: Cetra LO 15 [4]; Movimento MM3023 [3]

1957 June 14. Teatro Comunale, Florence (live performance)

Mario Del Monaco (*ten*) Ernani; Anita Cerquetti (*sop*) Elvira; Ettore Bastianini (*bar*) Carlo; BC Silva; Maggio Musicale Fiorentino Chorus and Orchestra/Dmitri Mitropoulos

Verdi: *Ernani*

CD: Melodram MEL27.016

1957 September 25–October 1. Opera House, Rome

Tito Gobbi (*bar*) Boccanegra; Victoria de los Angeles (*sop*) Amelia; Giuseppe Campora (*ten*) Gabriele; BC Fiesco; Walter Monachesi (*bar*) Paolo; Rome Opera Chorus and Orchestra/Gabriele Santini

Verdi: *Simone Boccanegra*

LP: HMV ALPS1634, ALP1635/6Y ALP 2067 (excs); SLS5090; Angel 3617CL; Seraphim IC6115

MC: TC-SLS5090

CD: CMS7 63513-2

1957 November. Salle Wagram, Paris

Alexandre Labinsky (*pf*)

Tchaikovsky: 'A tear trembles', Op. 6/4

45: HMV 7ER5221. PM 7ERF196

1957 November 26–December 18. Salle Mutualité, Paris

Teresa Stich-Randall (*sop*) Antonida; Melanie Bugarinović (*mez*) Vanya; Nicolai Gedda (*ten*) Sobinin; BC Susanin; Belgrade Opera Chorus; Lamoureux Orchestra/Igor Markevitch

Glinka: *A Life for the Tsar*

LP: HMV ALP1613/5; PM FALP505/7

CD: CMS7 69698-2

1958 May 12. Royal Opera House, Covent Garden

Gré Brouwenstijn (*sop*) Elisabetta; Fedora Barbieri (*mez*) Eboli; Jon Vickers (*ten*) Don Carlos; Tito Gobbi (*bar*) Rodrigo; BC Philip II; Michael Langdon (*bass*) Grand Inquisitor; Joseph Rouleau (*bass*) The Monk; Jeannette Sinclair (*sop*) Tebaldo; Robert Allman (*bar*) Herald; Edgar Evans (*ten*) Count of Lerma; Ava June (*sop*) Celestial Voice; Royal Opera House Chorus and Orchestra/Carlo Maria Giulini

Verdi: *Don Carlos*

LP: Paragon DSV52008

1958 September. Salle Mutualité

Alexandre Labinsky (*pf*)

Rachmaninov: 'He took all from me', Op 26/2; 'All things pass by', Op 26/15; 'Christ is risen', Op 26/6; 'The dream', Op 8/5; 'Fate', Op

21/1; 'O thou, my field', Op 4/5; 'How fair this spot', Op 21/7; 'Loneliness', Op 21/6; 'Morning', Op 4/2; 'Night is mournful', Op 26/12; 'Sing not to me, beautiful maiden', Op 4/4; 'Oh no, I beg you, forsake me not', Op 4/1; 'I have grown fond of sorrow', Op 8/4; 'I beg for mercy', Op 26/8; 'When yesterday we met', Op 26/13; 'How everyone loves thee', Op 14/6

  LP: HMV ALP1830. PM FALP569

1958 September 23–October 9. Salle Mutualité, Paris
 Victoria de los Angeles (*sop*) Marguerite; Nicolai Gedda (*ten*) Faust; Ernest Blanc (*bar*) Valentin; BC Méphistophélès; Liliane Berton (*sop*) Siébel; Rita Gorr (*mez*) Marthe; Paris Opera Chorus and Orchestra/André Cluytens

  Gounod: *Faust*
   45: 7ER5204 (s) RES4290; 7ER5212 (s) RES4296; 7ER5223 (s) RES4305
   LP: HMV ALP1721/4 (s) ASD307/10. (s) SLS816, ASD2559 (excs); PM ASDF101/4; Capitol GDR7154 (s) SGDR7154; Angel (s) SDL3622, (s) S-36948 (exc), S-35827 (excs)
   MC: TC-SLS816
   CD: EMI CMS7 69983-2; Angel CDMC 69983

1959 May. Salle Wagram, Paris
 Alexander Labinsky (*pf*)
  Bulgarian folksongs: 'Little Aichinka'; 'Wounded Soul'; 'Heaven is sleeping'
   45: HMV 7ER5221; PM 7ERF196
  Tchaikovsky: 'No response or word of greeting', Op. 28/5
   45: HMV 7ER5221; PM 7ERF196

1959 August 17–29 and October 4. Opera House, Rome
 Shakeh Vartenissian (*sop*); Fiorenza Cossotto (*mez*); Eugenio Fernandi (*ten*); BC; Rome Opera Chorus and Orchestra/Tullio Serafin
  Verdi: Requiem Mass
   LP: HMV ALP1775/6 (s) ASD353/4, (s) SXDW3055, PM ASDF211/2; Regal SREG 2042/3
   MC: TC-SXDW3055

1959 September & October and 1960 April. Salle Wagram
 Alexandre Labinsky (*pf*); *Gaston Marchesini (*vc*)
  Tchaikovsky: 'Don Juan's Serenade', Op 38/1; 'The mild stars shone for us', Op 60/12*; 'Child's Song', Op 54/16; 'Night', Op 60/9;

'Cradle Song', Op 16/1; 'Night', Op 73/2*; 'Do not ask', Op 57/3; 'As they kept on saying', 'Fool', Op 25/6; 'To sleep', Op 27/1; 'Disappointment', Op 65/2; 'The Canary', Op 25/4; 'None but the weary heart', Op 6/6*ª; 'Again, as before, alone', Op 73/6; 'A Legend: Christ in His garden', Op 54/5

> LP: HMV ALP1793 (s) ASD390; PM FALP569 (s) ASDF144; ªHMV YKM5004

1960 August 1. Salzburg Festival

Sena Jurinac (*sop*) Elisabetta; Regina Resnik (*mez*) Eboli; Eugenio Fernandi (*ten*) Don Carlos; Ettore Bastianini (*bar*) Rodrigo; BC Philip II; Raffaele Arié (*bass*) Grand Inquisitor; Nicola Zaccaria (*bass*) The Monk; Vienna State Opera Chorus; Vienna Philharmonic Orchestra/Nello Santi

> Verdi: *Don Carlos*
> LP: Melodram MEL

1961 July 2–11. Teatro alla Scala, Milan

Antonietta Stella (*sop*) Elisabetta; Fiorenza Cossotto (*mez*) Eboli; Flaviano Labò (*ten*) Don Carlos; Ettore Bastianini (*bar*) Rodrigo: BC Philip II; Ivo Vinco (*bass*) Grand Inquisitor; Alessandro Maddalena (*bass*) The Monk; Teatro alla Scala Chorus and Orchestra, Milan/Gabriele Santini

> Verdi: *Don Carlos*:
> LP: LPM18760/3 (s) SLPM138760/3; (s) 2740 197; (s) 2562 015/8 LPEM19274 (s) SLPEM136274 (excs)
> Ella giammai m'amò … Dormiro sol
> 45: EPL30460
> LP: SLPEM136528. 2548 280

1962 June & September. Salle Wagram, Paris

*Gaston Marchesini (*vc*); Alexandre Labinsky (*pf*)

> Glinka: 'Ah, you darling, lovely girl'; 'Do not say the heart is sick'*; 'Doubt'*; 'Elegy'*; *Farewell to Petersburg*: No 2, 'Hebrew Song', No 5, 'Cradle Song'*, No 10, 'The Lark'; 'Grandpa, the girls once told me'; 'How sweet to be with thee'; 'I remember the wonderful moment'; 'The midnight review'; 'What, young beauty'; 'Where is our rose?'*
> LP: HMV ALP1996 (s) ASD547; PM FALP776 (s) ASDF776

1962 September 4–21. Salle Wagram, Paris

Evelyn Lear (*sop*) Marina; Dimiter Uzunov (*ten*) Dmitri; BC Boris, Pimen and Varlaam; John Lanigan (*ten*) Shuisky; Anton Diakov (*bass*)

Rangoni; Jacques Mars (*bass*) Shchelkalov; Kiril Dulguerov (*ten*) The
Simpleton; Belgrade Opera Chorus; Paris Conservatoire Orchestra/
André Cluytens

Mussorgsky: *Boris Godunov*

LP: HMV AN110/13 (s) SAN110/14, ALP2257 (s) ASD2257
(excs), ALP2025 (s) ASD574 (exc), ASD2559 (exc); Angel
3633DL (s) SDL3633; 36172 (s) S-36172 (excs); Electrola (s)
1C 165 0009/12. SME80924 (excs)

CD: EMI CDC7 47993; Angel CDCC 47993.

1962 December 1. Teatro Comunale, Florence (live performance)

BC Attila; Gian Giacomo Guelfi (*bar*) Ezio; Margherita Roberti (*sop*)
Odabella; Gastone Limarilli (*ten*) Foresto; Franco Franchi (*ten*)
Uldino; Mario Frosini (*bass*) Leone; Teatro Comunale Chorus and
Orchestra, Florence/Bruno Bartoletti

Verdi: *Attila*

LP: Movimento MM3018 [2]

1963 February and 1964 April

Paris Conservatoire Orchestra/André Cluytens; Alexandre Labinsky
(*pf*) Vladimir Zampolsky (*pf*)

Rimsky-Korsakov: 'The upas tree'. Op 49/1; 'Across the midnight
sky', Op 40/2; 'Zuleika's Song', Op 26/4; 'Hebrew Song', Op 7/2;
'Withered flower', Op 51/3; 'I waited for thee in the grotto', Op
40/4; 'Slowly drag my days', Op 51/1; 'The sea is tossing', Op 46/3;
'The messenger', Op 4/2; 'The prophet', Op 49/2; 'The pine and
the palm', Op 3/1; 'Quiet is the blue sea', Op 50/3[a]; 'Quietly
evening falls', Op 4/4; 'On the hills of Georgia', Op 3/4; 'The rainy
day has waned', Op 51/5

LP: PM FALP835 (s) ASDF835; [a]HMV ASD2559

1963 April 22–24. Kingsway Hall

Philharmonia Orchestra/Jerzy Semkov

Borodin: *Prince Igor*: Konchak's aria

Gluck; *Iphigénie en Aulide*: O Diane impitoyable (sung in Italian)

Verdi: *Atilla*: Uldino! ... Mentre gonfiarsi[a]

Verdi: *Don Carlos*: Ella giammai m'amò[a]

LP: ALP2025 (s) ASD574, [a]ASD2559; Angel 36172 (s)
S-36172

CD: CDM7 69542-2

1966 May. Salle Wagram

Constantin Chekerliiski (*bar*) Igor; BC Galitsky, Konchak; Todor
Todorov (*ten*) Vladimir; Kyril Dulguerov (*ten*) Eroshka; Alexei
Milkovsky (*bass*) Skula; Luben Mihailov (*ten*) Ovlur; Julia Wiener
(*sop*) Yaroslavna; Reni Penkova (*contr*) Konchakova; Radka Gaeva
(*sop*) Nurse; Sofia National Opera Chorus and Orchestra/Jerzy
Semkow

    Borodin: *Prince Igor* [omits Act 3]
        LP: Angel (s) SCL3714, (s) S-36588 (excs); EMI (s) CAN176/8;
        HMV (s) ASD2345 (excs), ASD2559 (exc)
        CD: EMI CMS7 63386-2

1966 October and 1967 October–November. Salle Mutualité
    [a]Maud-Martin Tortelier (*cello*); [b] Alexandre Tcherepnin. [c]Jeanne Reiss
(*pfs*); [d]Lamoureux Orchestra/Georges Tzipine
    Borodin: 'Those folk'[d]; 'Song of the dark forest'[b]; 'From my tears'[b];
'The sea princess'[b]; 'The pretty girl no long loves me'[ab]; 'The magic
garden'[b]; 'Arabian melody'[b]; 'The false note'[b*]; 'The beautiful fisher
maiden'[ab]; 'Listen to my song, little friend'[ab]; 'The sleeping princess'[b];
'Pride'[b]; 'For the shores of thy far native land'[d*]; 'The sea'[c]; 'Why art
thou so early, dawn?'[b]; 'My songs are poisoned'[b]
        LP: PM 2C 063 10147; *HMV ASD2559
        CD: CMS7 63386-2

1966 Italian Radio Studios. Milan (broadcast performance)
    Bruno Prevedi (*ten*) Ernani; Montserrat Caballé (*sop*) Elvira; Peter
Glossop (*bar*) Carlo; BC Silva; Mirella Fiorentino (*mez*) Giovanna;
Franco Ricciardi (*ten*) Riccardo; Giuseppe Modesti (*bass*) Jago; Milan
RAI Chorus and Orchestra/Gianandrea Gavazzeni
    Verdi: *Ernani*
        CD: Nuova Era 2359/60

1967 March, April & October. Salle Wagram
    Alexandre Tcherepnin (*pf*); Lamoureux Orchestra/Georges Tzipine
        Balakirev: 'Dawn'; 'The yellow leaf trembles'; 'Hebrew melody';
        'Song of Selim'; 'The knight'; 'The wilderness'; 'Intonation';
        'Nocturne'; 'Look, my friend'[a]; 'The dream'; 'The pine-tree';
        'November the seventh'[a]; 'Always'; 'The dream'
        LP: PM 2C 063 10149; [a]HMV ASD2559

1967 October–November. Salle Mutualité
    Janine Reiss, Alexandre Zampolsky (*pfs*)
        Cui: 'The love of a dying man', Op. 5/2; 'Berceuse'; 'Song of Mary',

Op. 55/2; 'The imprisoned knight', Op. 55/7; 'The sky is chilled'; 'The plot', Op. 55/6; 'Longing', Op. 57/25ª; 'In memory of V.V. Stassov', Op. 86/24; 'Album leaf', Op. 86/20; 'Be a Teuton'; 'Hither', Op. 54/9; 'Later a song', Op. 5/3; 'Excuse me!', Op. 5/5; 'The prophet', Op. 55/3; 'The dreamers'; 'The statue at Tsarskoie Selo', Op. 57/17ª; 'The tomb and the rose', Op. 32/3

  LP: PM 2C 063 10148; ªHMV ASD2559

1968 May 7. Teatro Comunale, Florence (live performance)

  Giorgio Merighi (*ten*) Robert; Renata Scotto (*sop*) Isabelle; Stefania Malagù (*mez*) Alice; Maggio Musicale Fiorentino Chorus and Orchestra/Nino Sanzogno

  Meyerbeer: *Robert le Diable* (sung in Italian)

  LP: MRF MRF20

  CD: Hunt CD549

1972 March 27 (plus one undated 'patch-up' session) Danmarks Radio Concert Hall, Copenhagen.

  BC Saul; Alexander Young (*ten*) David; Elisabeth Söderström (*sop*) Michal; Willy Hartmann (*ten*) Jonathan; Michael Langdon (*bass*) Samuel; Sylvia Fisher (*sop*) Witch of Endor; Kim Borg (*bass*) Abner; Danish Radio Chorus and Symphony Orchestra/Jascha Horenstein

  Nielsen: *Saul and David*

  LP: Unicorn (s) RHS343/5

  CD: DKPCD9086/7

1975 June 9–13 and 1976 August 17. Studio des Dames, Paris

  'Russian Romances & Folksongs'

  Alyabiev: 'The Nightingale' Anon (arr Gesine Trefuhr): 'Grief, affliction, all hope is gone'; 'Oh pain, pass away'; 'Soon the sadness will be gone'; 'Nastasya'; 'I am grieved that thou canst not see into my heart'; 'Do not touch me, lest I turn to flame'; 'How the wind howls in the chimney'

  Anon (arr Georges Streha): 'Alas, fate, oh bitter fate'; 'Masha may not go down to the river'; 'Two guitars are sadly playing'; 'Where the eternal snow lies on the Kazbek'; 'Come, my guitar, play on'

  LP: DG 2536 115

  MC: DG 3336 115

1977 Sofia

  Alexander Nevsky Cathedral Choir, Sofia/Angel Konstantinov

  Chesnokov: 'Evening sacrifice'

Zinoviev: 'We hymn Thee'
Kochetov: 'Blessed is the man'
Hristov: 'Praise ye the name of God'; 'Nunc dimittis'
Dinev: 'The Judicious Villain'
Strnumski: 'The Great Glorification'
Lyubimov: 'Blessed is the man'
Bortnyansky: 'Grant, O Lord'
    LP: HMV ASD3513; Angel S-37479; PM 2C 069 60552
    MC: HMV TC-ASD3513
1979 Sofia
  Svetoslav Obretenov National Chorus; Bulgarian Radio Symphony Orchestra/Ettore Gracis
    Beethoven: *Fidelio*: 'Ha, Welch' ein Augenblick'
    Gluck: *Iphigénie en Aulide*: Con le mie guardie ... O tu la cosa mia più cara
    Monteverdi: *L'Incoronazione di Poppea*: 'Solitudine amata'
    Mozart: 'Così dunque tradisci'; ... 'Aspri rimorsi atroci', K432
    Rameau: *Dardanus*: Marstre affieux
    Verdi: *Macbeth*: Come dal ciel precipità
      LP: Forlane UM4508
      MC: Forlane UMK4508
1979/80 Bulgarian Concert Hall, Sofia
  Irina Shtiglich (*pf*), Ivan Drenikov (*pf*)
  Grechaninov: 'Night voices'; 'Don't ask why'; 'In the dark copse'; 'Scarcely had I heard the song'; 'A sharp axe'; 'In light slumber'; 'A little flower'; 'Like an angel'; 'Nightmare'; 'A cuckoo'; 'I do not know'; 'I dreamt ...'; 'Grim and evil'; 'Autumn motifs'; 'Kolodniki'; 'Epitaph II'
    LP: Balkanton BKA 11754

May 1991